BUT

First staged at the Criterion Theatre in 1971, *Butley* is a play about a university lecturer, Ben Butley, who shares his office and his flat with a former star pupil, Joey, now also a teacher. On the day when the play takes place Butley faces both the ultimate breakdown of his marriage and of his intense friendship with Joey. Butley's painful discoveries are made against a background of petty university politics and unease about student dissent. He greets them with a blistering torrent of repartee and rhetoric.

'Butley . . . could well join that distinguished gallery of human debris represented by Willie Loman, Jimmy Porter and Bill Maitland in post-war drama. . . . What is so wondrous about a play so basically defeatist and hurtful is its ability to be funny. The stark, unsentimental approach to the homosexual relationship, the cynical send-up of academic life, the sceptical view of the teacher-pupil associations are all stunningly illuminated by continuous explosions of sardonic, needling, feline, vituperative and civilised lines.

Milton Shulman in the *Evening Standard*.

The photograph on the front of the cover shows Alan Bates and Richard O'Callaghan in a scene from the Criterion production and is reproduced by courtesy of John Haynes. The photograph on the back of the cover is reproduced by courtesy of Beryl Gray.

by the same author

Plays

SLEEPING DOG

WISE CHILD

DUTCH UNCLE

SPOILED

THE IDIOT

OTHERWISE ENGAGED
and other plays

DOG DAYS

Novels

COLMAIN

LITTLE PORTIA

SIMPLE PEOPLE

A COMEBACK FOR STARK
(The last title published under
the pseudonym Hamish Reade)

Simon Gray

BUTLEY

EYRE METHUEN

LONDON

First published in 1971
by Methuen & Co Ltd
Reprinted 1975 and 1977
by Eyre Methuen
11 New Fetter Lane,
London EC4P 4EE
Copyright © 1971 by Simon Gray
Printed Offset Litho in Great Britain
by Cox & Wyman Ltd
Fakenham, Norfolk
ISBN 0413 34060 0

ACKNOWLEDGEMENT

The lines from T. S. Eliot's *Collected Poems* 1909–1962 quoted on pages 34 and 76–7 are reprinted by kind permission of Messrs Faber and Faber Ltd. The lines by Beatrix Potter, from *Cecily Parsley's Nursery Rhymes* and *Appley Dappley's Nursery Rhymes,* quoted on pages 10, 11, 16, 45 and 77 are reprinted by kind permission of Messrs Frederick Warne & Co., Ltd.

To the staff and students,
past, present and future,
of the English Department,
Queen Mary College, London

BUTLEY was first presented on 14th July 1971, at the Criterion Theatre by Michael Codron with the following cast:

BEN BUTLEY	Alan Bates
JOSEPH KEYSTON	Richard O'Callaghan
MISS HEASMAN	Brenda Cavendish
EDNA SHAFT	Mary Wimbush
ANNE BUTLEY	Colette O'Neil
REG NUTTALL	Michael Byrne
MR GARDNER	George Fenton

Directed by Harold Pinter

ACT ONE

An office in a College of London University. About 10 in the morning.
The office is badly decorated (white walls, greying, plaster boards)
with strip lighting. There are two desks opposite each other, each
with a swivel chair. BEN's *desk, left, is a chaos of papers, books,*
detritus. JOEY's *desk, right, is almost bare. Behind each desk is a*
bookcase. Again, BEN's *is chaotic with old essays and mimeographed*
sheets scattered among the books, while JOEY's *is neat, not many*
books on the shelves. On each desk there is a table lamp and in front of
each desk a hard chair. There is one telephone, on BEN's *desk, the*
flex of which is long enough to reach JOEY's *desk. There are a few*
hard-backed chairs around the walls, and one armchair, in BEN's
corner of the room. On the wall is a blown-up picture (photograph)
of T. S. Eliot, with a smear across it and one of its corners curled.
The panels to the office door are frosted glass, behind which people,
when they approach, are dimly seen.

BEN *is a heavy smoker, and should smoke more frequently than the*
text indicates. JOEY *does not smoke.*

As the curtain rises, BEN *enters, in a plastic raincoat, which he takes*
off and throws into his chair. He has a lump of cotton wool on his
chin, from a particularly nasty shaving-cut. He goes to his chair, sits
down, looks around as if searching for something, shifts uncomfortably,
pulls the plastic mac out from under him, searches through its pockets,
takes out half a banana, a bit squashed, then throws the raincoat
over to JOEY's *desk. He takes a bite from the banana, removes it from*
the peel and drops the last piece onto his desk. Then he throws the
peel onto JOEY's *desk. He slumps into his chair – a long pause – the*
telephone rings.

BEN. Butley, English. Hello, James, have a nice break? (*A pause –*
he mouths a curse.) Sorry, James, I can't talk now – I'm right in the
middle of a tutorial – 'bye.

Then he touches the cottonwool and tries to pull it off. He lets out an exclamation. Touches his chin, looks at his finger.

(*In an undertone*). Bugger!

He gets up, looks under his desk, drags out a bulging briefcase from which he pulls an opened bag of cotton wool. He delves into his briefcase again and takes out a tin of Nescafé. He shines the base on his sleeve, then holds it to his chin as if it were a mirror. He tries to put the cotton wool on, then switches on the light. It doesn't come on. He sticks the cotton wool on. He shoves the Nescafé tin back into his briefcase and stuffs the cotton wool into his jacket pocket. He goes across to the main switch and flicks it on. The strip lighting flickers into brilliance. He checks the cotton wool using the glass door of his bookcase as a mirror, then, unable to bear the striplight, flicks it off again. He goes across to JOEY's *desk and tries the lamp. It comes on. He wipes stray wisps of cotton wool from his fingers with the banana skin, then drops it into the clean ashtray on* JOEY's *desk. He switches off* JOEY's *lamp and carries it across to his desk. There is a shape at the door, then a knock.*

Bugger! Just a minute!

He carries his lamp across to JOEY's. *The door opens cautiously.*

A minute I said. (*He goes to the door and checks it with his hand.*) Hello.

STUDENT (*off*). Hello.

BEN (*after a pause*). Can I help you?

STUDENT (*off*). Well, it's my tutorial. On Wordsworth. 'The Prelude'.

BEN. Oh. No, I can't give tutorials during the first week after the break I'm afraid. Too much administration.

STUDENT (*off*). Oh? When should I come then?

BEN. Come at the same hour of the same day of next week.

STUDENT (*off*). Next week?

BEN. Next week. If we keep to our time-table we'll know where we are, won't we? All right? (*He closes the door.*)

He goes back to his desk, sits down and takes out of his pocket a copy of 'Cecily Parsley'.

'The Prelude'.

He shudders, then turns a page, reaches for the light, clicks it. Nothing happens. He gets up and goes over to JOEY's desk, tries the light, it comes on. He sighs. He sits down in JOEY's chair, opens one of his drawers, props his feet in it, and settles down to read.
JOEY comes in with a briefcase. He puts it down on his desk, clears the banana peel into the waste-paper basket, picks BEN's raincoat up, carries it over to the peg, puts the desk lamps back on their respective desks. He turns on his table light – it comes on.

Good morning.
JOEY. Good morning.
BEN. Nice to see you.
JOEY. Nice to be seen. What's the matter with your chin?
BEN. I'm trying to cultivate cotton wool on it. Your own is shining pleasantly, what did you have to work with, a razor?
JOEY. What did *you* use?
BEN. Anne left one behind. Behind the fridge, to be exact. So either mice have taken up shaving, or that stubble was sheared from her calves. I thought of mounting a tuft in a locket. You needn't have taken the only one we have.
JOEY. It also happens to be the only one I have.
BEN. Couldn't you have shared Ted's? It's no pleasure slicing open my chin with my estranged wife's razor blade. The symbolism may be deft, but the memory still smarts.
JOEY. I didn't mean to take it, in point of fact. I put it in the bag **without** thinking.

BEN. Lust is no excuse for thoughtlessness. And where is your bag? (*He stands up and peers round for it.*)

JOEY. What? Oh, I left it with Reg.

BEN. Reg? Who's Reg? (*He perches on the front of his own desk with his feet up on a chair and lights a cigarette.* JOEY *hastily occupies the vacated desk chair.*)

JOEY. Reg is his name.

BEN. Whose name?

JOEY. Ted's.

BEN. Reg is Ted's name?

JOEY. The one you call Ted is the one I call Reg. He calls himself Reg too.

BEN. How sweet.

JOEY. In fact, everybody calls him Reg except you. You call him Ted.

BEN. Why do I do that, I wonder.

JOEY. To embarrass me.

BEN. Oh yes, that must be it. (*Pause.*) Did you have a good week-end?

JOEY. It was all right. (*Pause.*) Have you seen James this morning?

BEN. Ah! Our Professor! He's just been hounding me on the telephone. He and Hazel spent most of the break in bed recovering from one of Hazel's gastric goulashes.

JOEY. Did he say anything? I mean, are there any details yet?

BEN. You want details of James' diarrhoea?

JOEY. You know what I mean. About my board.

BEN. Ah. About your board. Now when is that, exactly?

JOEY. A fortnight tomorrow.

BEN. Indeed? A fortnight tomorrow? Mmmm. Where the hell is it? (*He begins to search in his desk drawers –* JOEY *comes over to him.*)

JOEY. What?

BEN. It's no real advance. (*Sits.*) But it's got some interesting things in it. Damn! Anyway –

  'How do you do, Mistress Pussy?

Mistress Pussy, how do you do?'
'I thank you kindly little dog,
I fare as well as you!'

JOEY. Did he say anything?

BEN. You're genuinely interested in this promotion of yours,
aren't you? Why? (*Little pause.*) No, he didn't say anything.
Your name didn't come up, and there's no reason that it should
until, in the normal course of events and strictly according to
the rules, the board is rigged, the strings are pulled, and it's
passed over for that of someone more closely related to the
Principal, or with more distinguished qualifications, I should
warn you that there are almost as many of the latter as of the
former.

Cecily Parsley lived in a pen,
And brewed good ale for gentlemen;
Gentlemen came every day.

(*Joey goes to his shelves and takes down a book.*)

Till Cecily Parsley ran away.
Why? (BEN *crosses to* JOEY.) Why has he got your bag?

JOEY. He happened to pick it up for me when we got off the train.

BEN. Not many young men are as gallant these days. You haven't
been home yet then?

JOEY. To the flat. No? (*He sits at his desk.*)

BEN. Ah. Why not?

JOEY. Because I didn't have time, obviously. (*He begins to correct
a set of essays from his briefcase.*)

BEN. I waited for you.

JOEY. Did you? Sorry.

BEN (*watches him*). You had a nice little mid-term break then, did
you?

JOEY. It was all right.

BEN. Well, are you going to tell me about it, or shall I probe and
pry?

JOEY. I'd rather let it slip out naturally, if I may?

BEN. But you're much more charming under interrogation. My natural force plays excitingly with your natural submissiveness. Or has your holiday changed you, as we say in the trade, radically? (*He opens* JOEY'*s briefcase.*) Ah-hah! I thought so! (*As* JOEY *looks up.*) Blake! Why is your briefcase bulging with Blake? (*He opens one of the books and takes out a piece of paper.*) What's this?

JOEY. I happen to be lecturing on him this half. (*He tries to take the book and notes from him.*) Kindly don't mess my notes up. Can I have it back, please?

BEN. Notes to whom? Reg?

What immortal hand or eye

Could frame thy fearful symmetry?

Ted is certainly quite symmetrical – in a burly sort of way.

Did he who made the lamb make thee?

Laughs.

JOEY. All right, all right, let's *be* infantile. (*He goes across to* BEN'*s desk and picks up his briefcase.*)

BEN (*drops* JOEY'*s book and notes, lunges across and grabs his own briefcase*). No, bags first go. I haven't unpacked it for weeks.

He opens it, as JOEY *returns to his marking. He pulls out an empty scotch bottle, then a red-covered manuscript.*

It's laid out like a film script. It must be an American M.A. thesis – Ah – 'Henry James and the Crucified Consciousness' – aaah.

BEN *wanders over to* JOEY'*s desk, pulls out a blue sock, puts the thesis down on* JOEY'*s desk, along with a few more papers, files, crumpled newspaper, the Nescafé tin and the briefcase itself.*

Now where's the other – there must be a pair –

JOEY (*picks up the thesis*). You mean you forgot to give his thesis back?

BEN. Not yet. So far I've forgotten to read it. Forgetting to give it back will come later. Failing Americans is a slow and

intricate ritual and that's what they come here for – the ritual –
aaah, here it is.

> BEN *takes out another sock. It is red. He picks up the blue. Looks
> at them.*

JOEY. Those are mine. Naturally.

BEN. Naturally you're very welcome. (*He tosses the socks at*
JOEY.) Personally I wouldn't be caught dead wearing a pair
like that. (*He lifts up his trousers, studies his socks.*)

JOEY. Those happen to be mine, too.

BEN. You really must give up buying cheap socks. I can feel a hole
growing around the toe.

JOEY (*savagely*). Perhaps if you bothered to cut your toe-nails –
(*He picks up the thesis and essays* BEN *has dropped.*)

BEN. Are we going to have a tantrum?

JOEY. The thing is to stop your rubbish creeping across to my
side of the room.

> *He makes as if to stack them neatly, then crams them savagely
> into* BEN's *shelves.*

Here, anyway. (*He goes back to his desk and continues marking.*)

BEN. *Are* we? I'd quite enjoy one.

JOEY. Would you?

BEN. Then I'll know you're back, you see. You've been a little
thin on presence so far.

JOEY. There's not enough room.

> BEN *sits down cross legged on the top of* JOEY's *desk and watches*
> JOEY. *He clears his throat delicately. He smiles genteely.*

BEN (*genteel*). I was just wondering if I might enquire as to how
your friend is, may I?

> JOEY *smiles.*

Hoh, h'I'm so glad.

JOEY *continues transcribing marks*.

May h'I hask, done all those, 'ave we?

He takes the essay JOEY *is holding*.

Ho, but you 'adn't done them last week 'ad you? Did you do them on the train, going h'up with your friend?

Shape at the door, BEN *doesn't notice*.

H'I h'always say that h'if h'a job's worth doing h'it's worth h'ignoring.

Knock on the door. BEN *turns, starts to move rapidly to it. When it opens,* MISS HEASMAN, *a pretty, competent-looking girl steps in*.

MISS HEASMAN. Oh, sorry, I was just wondering when my tutorials are.

BEN. Same as last term, except of course for this week.

MISS HEASMAN. You didn't take me last term. My name is Heasman, Carol Heasman. I'm replacing Mrs Grainger.

BEN. Mrs Grainger?

MISS HEASMAN. Yes. She said she didn't get to see you often, owing to administrative tangles.

BEN. Mrs Grainger got into administrative tangles?

MISS HEASMAN. No, you were busy with them.

BEN. If only they'd let us get on with it and teach. (*Laughs.*) Anyway, you'd better come at the same hours as Mrs Grainger, all right?

MISS HEASMAN. I expect so. What were they?

BEN. Could you find out from Mrs Grainger, please?

MISS HEASMAN. I'll try.

BEN. Thank you. (*He holds the door wider.* MISS HEASMAN *goes out.* BEN *returns to his desk.*) I didn't care for that one at all, there was an air of mad devotion about her that reminds me of my wife's mother, the mad monk. (*Looking at* JOEY, *who is still transcribing marks.* JOEY *tries to go on working. In a normal tone after a pause.*) You're in trouble, Joey.

JOEY. What? (*He looks up.*)

BEN. I'm sorry. I've been wondering how to tell you. But as you've still got a fortnight before the board. (*Sits. Pause.*) A member of the department has his knife out.

JOEY. Who?

BEN. That pre-break meeting we had – the one you had to leave early – to meet Reg?

JOEY. Yes. Well?

BEN. The contemporary books list?

JOEY. Yes. Well, go on.

BEN. On the face of it, you were very adroit. You didn't actually support me, but you indicated a certain, attitude shall we say? By coughing into my speeches with dialectical authority. You wouldn't have thought that so genteel a rhetorical device could give offence. On the face of it. Eh?

JOEY. But who – who did I offend?

BEN (*gets up and perches on the front of his desk again*). First of all who proposed that a contemporary novels list – Burroughs, Genet, Roth, etc. – be added to our syllabus?

JOEY. You did.

BEN. And who opposed it?

JOEY. Everybody else. Except – me.

BEN. Who won?

JOEY. We – you did. They gave way in the end – didn't they?

BEN (*sinisterly*). Oh yes, it was passed unanimously – but I happen to know that one person – one powerful person there – resented *our* victory and blamed you – yes, you – for it.

JOEY. But this is ridiculous! It's absolutely – I scarcely said anything anyway.

BEN. Exactly. But this person was hoping – was *relying* – on you to oppose that book list with every cell in your body.

JOEY. Ben, please – eh?

BEN. Think, child, think! Who had most to lose by that list being passed? Who is *most* affected?

JOEY. Nobody. Nobody at all. You're the one who's going to teach it, they'll be *your* lectures, *your* seminars, *your* tutorials . . .

BEN (*after a long pause, as* JOEY *realizing, looks at him*). Exactly. Precisely. Absolutely. Fool! Imbecile! Traitor! Lackey! – I wouldn't be caught dead reading those books. And you know how it exhausts me to teach books I haven't read. Why didn't you oppose me?

JOEY. It's your own fault. Your instructions were quite clear.

BEN. Haven't you heard of a sub-text? It's very fashionable now, In fact, I remember advising you to use the word twice in every paper when I was guiding you through your finals. (*He goes to examine him.*) But what's the matter, dear? You're looking a little peaky around the gills, wherever they are? Were you frightened, a trifle? You needn't be – you played the toad to perfection. (*He returns to his desk.*)

JOEY. Is there a sub-text to that? Or can I take it as straight abuse?

BEN. It's straight abuse. Can you take it?

JOEY (*trembling slightly*). No, not any longer. (*He gets up, and begins to pack his briefcase.*)

BEN. Where are you going?

JOEY. To the library.

BEN. Why?

JOEY. I've got a lecture at twelve.

BEN. But you're not running away from me so soon?

JOEY. And there are a few things on my Herrick I've got to dig up. (*He goes to the door –* BEN *cuts him off.*)

BEN. Dig up! (*Laughs.*)

    Diggory, diggory Delvet

    Little old man in black velvet

    He digs and he delves

    You can see for yourselves

    The holes dug by Diggory Delvet.

It is velvet, isn't it, this jacket? (*Fingering it.*)

JOEY *tugs his sleeve away.*

No, don't flounce.

They stand staring at each other.

You were due back last night, remember?

JOEY. Did it make any difference?

BEN. In that I spent the evening expecting you.

JOEY. In point of fact, I said I'd be back either last night or this morning.

BEN. Also you didn't phone.

JOEY. I was only in Leeds for four days. Of course I didn't phone.

BEN. Why not? Language difficulties? I reserved a table at Bianchi's. I was going to take us out.

JOEY (*after a pause*). I'm sorry.

BEN *shrugs. They each return to their desks.*

It just didn't occur to me –

BEN. It doesn't matter.

JOEY. I'm sure I said –

BEN. Yes, yes, I expect you did. I assumed you were coming back, that's all. And as I spent four days on the phone to people who weren't there – bugger! (*He sits down at his desk.*) I'm sorry. All right? And if that doesn't satisfy you, Edna thinks well of you, and James is more than happy.

JOEY. How do you know?

BEN. These things slip out. Under my persistent questionings.

JOEY. Edna's actually very important, isn't she? (*He goes across to* BEN *and sits on the hard chair in front of* BEN's *desk.*)

BEN. It depends rather on the context.

JOEY. I mean in terms of influence –

BEN. You mean in terms of promotion?

JOEY. Well – (*Grins.*)

BEN. She'll certainly sit on your board, yes. Don't worry. You'll get your lectureship. Then you'll be safe for ever.

JOEY. I like Edna, in point of fact. No, really. We came in on the tube together this morning. She was telling me about her Byron –

BEN. Can we actually – do you mind? – not discuss either Edna or Byron but most of all Edna on Byron, for purely private reasons just at the moment. The thought of them weighs on my spirit. (*Pause.*) Tell me, while you were amusing yourselves in Leeds, I saw a film on television about a publisher who hates himself. I've been meaning to ask you – does Ted hate himself?

JOEY. He quite likes himself, actually.

BEN. I don't blame him. He seemed an amiable sort of chap the one time I met him, even though his mouth was full of symbolic sausage and his fist around a tankard of something foaming symbolically. I had the impression that most people would like him. And as he seemed exactly like most people, only from the North, ergo, he'd be favourably disposed towards himself only more so, or not? (*Smiles.*)

JOEY *also smiles.*

Tell me, does he ever discuss his work with you? Or does he leave it behind him at the office? When you go around for one of those little dinners, does he put his feet up, perhaps, while you slave away over a hot stove, or does he do the cooking? No, I don't mean to probe – or am I prying? For instance, in our Professor's ménage Hazel rips the meat apart with saw-edged knives while James brews up sauces from *Guardian* headlines. In my ménage, when I had one – remember? – Anne under-grilled the chops and over-boiled the peas while I drank the wine and charted my dropping sugar count. Now that you and I are sharing my life again I open the tins and you stir the Nescafé again, just as we always used to do, those evenings, at least, when you're not cooking for Reg or Reg isn't cooking for you –

which, arriving where we began, does it happen to be? and if it's the former, why, now I think of it, have you never cooked for me, do you think?

JOEY. He does the cooking, in point of fact.

BEN. Christ I feel awful. (*Pause.*) Do you know, all the time you were away, I didn't have one telephone call. I consider that very frightening. Not even from Tom.

JOEY. Oh. (*Pause.*) I thought you found his company intolerable.

BEN. But one likes, as they say, to be asked. Also one likes people to be consistent, otherwise one will start coming adrift. At least this one will. (*Stands up.*) Also how does one know whether Tom is still the most boring man in London unless he phones in regularly to confirm it. This is the fourth week running he's kept me in suspense. He and Reg have a lot in common, haven't they? (*Pause. He sits on the desk.*)

JOEY (*drily*). Really?

BEN. Didn't Ted do his National Service with the Gurkhas?

JOEY. I really can't remember. I've never been very interested in Ted's – Reg's – military career, which was anyway about a decade ago. (*He goes back to his own desk.* BEN *follows him.*)

BEN. Oh, but the experience lives on for us through our born raconteurs – and Ted is something of a raconteur, isn't he? That magnificent anecdote of his – surely you remember?

JOEY. No. (*He picks up his briefcase and moves towards the door.*) I really must get to the library –

BEN. No, wait. (*Blocks his way.*) You repeated it to me. About the Gurkha and the bowl of soup. (*He holds up two fists.*) I don't know if I can do your imitation of his accent – woon day Chef was in ta kitchen – is that close? – stirring ta soup wi' his elbows – wan in coom a little tyke –

JOEY. I remember.

BEN. I was sure you would. Your imitation of Reg made me laugh so much that I was prepared to overlook its cruelty. Anyway my point was simply that Tom's a great National Service bore, too. There's that six volume novel he's writing about it – that's something else. Yes. He's stopped showing me his drafts. (*He goes back to his desk.*)

JOEY. The last time he brought one around you dropped it in the bath.

BEN. It! He brought around seventeen exercise books, of which I dropped a mere three into the bath. No, I don't like his silence. It's sinister.

JOEY. Well, you could always phone him up. (*He starts for the door again.*)

BEN. I haven't finished. (*He comes over, takes* JOEY's *briefcase from him and sits in* JOEY's *desk chair.*)

JOEY. I must do something on this bloody lecture.

BEN. Why? You're looking furtive. Why are you looking furtive?

JOEY. I'm not looking at all furtive.

BEN. Have you seen Tom recently?

JOEY. No. No I haven't.

BEN. When did you last hear from him?

JOEY (*shrugs*). Perhaps he's busy.

BEN. Of course he's busy. He's too dull to be anything else, the question is, why has he stopped being busy with me? (*He returns to his own desk and sits on the hard chair.*) Do you think he's dropped me. His attentions have been slackening since my marriage broke up, now I come to think of it.

JOEY (*carefully*). He's very fond of Anne, isn't he?

BEN (*laughs*). That's an idea. I must find out whether he's been hounding *her*.

JOEY. But Anne – (*Stops.*) She likes him, doesn't she? I mean, I always thought – had the impression that she was fond of him?

BEN. Oh, I expect she became addicted. She took up all my vices except drinking, smoking and you. She never cared for you. Did you know that?

JOEY. I had my suspicions. Thank you for confirming them.

BEN. She said that Tom became a school teacher because he had to prove, after three years of being taught by me at Cambridge, that education was still a serious affair. Whereas you wanted to get back to your old college here and with me because you were incapable of outgrowing your early influences. Nursery dependence. This analysis was based crudely on the fact that you are homosexual. She also said you were sly and pushing, and that she didn't trust you an inch.

JOEY. You never told me this before.

BEN. You never asked me before.

JOEY. I didn't ask you now, either.

BEN. I know. But I got tired of waiting. (*Pause.*) Do *you* like *her*?

JOEY. I thought we were friends.

BEN. I'm sure you still are. (*He sits in the armchair,* JOEY's *briefcase tucked under his arm.*) She just can't stand you, that's all. Something about you gives her the creeps, was her word. Creeps. (*Laughs.*) What's the matter? Are you upset?

JOEY *shakes his head.*

You shouldn't be. It was just her way of getting at me. Don't you see how I emerge? As someone whose protégé is a creep? But *I* didn't take offence. I don't see why you should. (*Pause.* JOEY *tries to take his case –* BEN *clutches it to him.*) Tell me, what does he do, Reg's dad?

JOEY *looks at him.*

(*Smiles.*) But we're not ashamed, are we?

JOEY (*pause.*) He owns a shop.

BEN. What sort of shop?

JOEY. Just a shop. (*He walks away from him.*)

BEN. Just a shop? Just a shop like Harrods, for example. What does he sell?

JOEY (*after a pause*). Meat, I think.

BEN. You think. Did you ever see the shop?

JOEY. Of course. Why?

BEN. Was there meat on display?

JOEY. Yes.

BEN. In that case he either owns a meat museum or if it was for sale you're quite right, he owns a shop that sells meat. He's what's called a butcher.

JOEY (*sits on the hard chair in front of* BEN's *desk*). That's right, he's a butcher.

BEN. Mmm huh. And do they live over their shop?

JOEY (*hesitates*). No. They live in um, in a place just outside Leeds, in point of fact.

BEN. In Point of Fact? And what sort of place is it, a Georgian terraced house, a Chippendale-style flat, a dug-out, a rural cottage; a bungalow!

JOEY. Yes. A bungalow.

BEN. A bungalow, eh? Now let's see, starting with the garden, do they have, say, plaster gnomes in the garden?

JOEY. And also much to your satisfaction, say, an electric fire with coals in it, and a sofa decorated with doilies and a revolving bookcase with the collected works of Mazo de la Roche –

BEN. In the garden? How witty!

JOEY. And their front door-bell plays a tune, can you believe that? (*Pause.*) They happen to be very nice people, nevertheless.

BEN. Nevertheless what?

JOEY (*emphatically*). Nevertheless they happen to be very nice people.

BEN (*sits on the edge of his desk, leaving* JOEY's *briefcase in the armchair*). What tune? (*Pause.*) Does Reg's mother work in the shop too?

JOEY. No.

BEN. Oh. Where is she then, in the day-time?

JOEY. Out.

BEN. Out where?

JOEY. Just out.

BEN. She has a job then?

JOEY. Yes.

BEN. And where does she do this job? On the streets?

JOEY. You could put it like that, yes.

BEN. What does she do? Sweep them?

JOEY. No.

BEN. She walks them?

JOEY. Yes, in point of fact.

BEN. The precise suburb is irrelevant. (*Pause.*) So Reg's mother is a prostitute.

JOEY *giggles, checks himself.*

JOEY. No, she's a – traffic warden.

BEN. She isn't! But what on earth did you do?

JOEY. Nothing in particular.

BEN. You went to a football match?

JOEY. Football match?

BEN. Hasn't it caught on there? Here in the South we place it slightly below music and well above theatre, in the cultural scale. Did you?

JOEY. What?

BEN. Go to any football matches?

JOEY. Well done. Yes we did. We went to a football match – and furthermore we wore rosettes, coloured scarves and special hats and carried rattles.

BEN. You didn't! (*Laughs.*) Rattles and rosettes? You didn't! You poor old sod. Why in Christ did you stay? (*Pause.*) All right then, why did he take you there? Is it like bringing one's latest girl back to the folks –?

JOEY. His friends back. He doesn't like people to know he's queer. A lot of the time he doesn't like me to know. But I suppose he probably took me there as a kind of compliment – and perhaps as a test.

BEN. To see if you could take him *au naturel*?

JOEY. That sounds reasonable, yes.

BEN. And could you?

JOEY. He's much more natural as a London publisher who knows all about food, and cooks marvellously. Much more natural and much more convincing.

BEN. But tell me – the butcher and the traffic warden – do they *know* –

JOEY. Know what?

A shape appears at the door. BEN *charges out as* MISS HEAS-MAN *knocks.*

BEN. Oops! Sorry!

MISS HEASMAN. Sorry!

BEN (*off*). Just dashing up to the Registrar's – some administrative tangle. Mrs Grainger isn't it?

MISS HEASMAN (*off*). Miss Heasman! I can't find Mrs Grainger but I'm very anxious for a session on *A Winter's Tale*.

BEN. Good God! Are you really? Well keep trying and perhaps by next week . . . I go up here. Goodbye.

BEN dodges back and surprises JOEY as he tries to leave.

. . . that you and Reg have it off together?

JOEY. Of course not. (*Shuts the door.*) And now I think I'd like to stop talking about it if you don't mind. I'm beginning to feel queasy.

BEN. Recollections of tripe and stout?

    Guilt Lord, I pray
    Answer thy servant's question!
    Is it guilt I feel
    Or is it indigestion?

Don't worry, *rognons au vin* at Bianchi's will calm the unsettled soul. (*He sits on his desk – lights a cigarette.*)

JOEY. Tonight you mean? For dinner?

BEN. I hardly fancy them for tea.

JOEY. Um, the thing is, I'm um going around to Reg's tonight. (*Pause.*) I – I didn't – I'm sorry, it just seemed impossible not to go, under the circumstances.

BEN. Mmm huh. (*Little pause.*) I'm willing to treat Reg if necessary.

JOEY. Well, you see Reg has already got our dinner.

BEN. Oh? And what's he got for your dinner?

JOEY (*laughs*). Well, kidneys, as a matter of fact. His father gave him some special – English kidneys. As a treat. Lamb's kidneys.

BEN. Mmm huh. (*Little pause.*)

JOEY. Sorry.

BEN. There's no problem. I'll get some more and Ted can cook them for me. (JOEY *goes back to his desk. Pause.*) What's the matter?

JOEY. I'd rather you didn't.

BEN. Mmm huh. May one ask why?

JOEY. It might be awkward.

BEN. Oh? May one wonder why?

JOEY. Perhaps he doesn't like you very much.

BEN. You surprise me. I thought he'd taken rather a fancy, on our one meeting.

JOEY (*sits*). On your one meeting you pretended you thought he was an Australian and addressed him as 'Cobber'. You also pretended you thought he was an interior decorator, in order to remind him of Ted, whom he knew to be his predecessor. You were also sick over his shoes. It was a terrible evening. He hated you.

BEN. You never told me this before.

JOEY. You never asked me before.

BEN. *That* was creepy. (*Pause.*) Anyway you exaggerate. The confusion over his national identity and profession lasted a mere twenty minutes at the beginning of the evening. It took me some twenty seconds to be sick over his shoes at the evening's end. The intervening hour was an unqualified success, in spite of the odd misunderstanding that developed into the occasional quarrel. Also you know very well that I'd taken up drinking again because I was still brooding over Anne's departure. I had what is called a drinking problem. I no longer have it.

JOEY. Let's face it Ben, you drink every night. Very heavily.

BEN. Exactly. There's no problem. I'm used to it again. (*Pause.*) Well, Joey?

JOEY *shrugs awkwardly.*

I might also be glad of a chance to make it up. I enjoy being on terms with your chaps. (*Pause.*) Also I don't fancy a fifth night of eating alone. (*Pause.*) Well?

JOEY. He won't want you to come.

BEN. Have you asked him?

JOEY. No.

BEN. Then why don't you? Come on. Let's find out. (*He picks up the telephone, and hands it to him.*) Well?

JOEY. He's not there.

BEN. How do you know, unless you try?

JOEY. He said he wouldn't be there until after lunch.

BEN *stares at him.*

He told me he had some things to do.

There is a shape at the door, not noticed by BEN *and* JOEY, *followed by a knock, and simultaneously* EDNA *comes in. She is in her late forties and carries a small pile of folders.*

EDNA. Hello, Ben. Joey.

BEN. Hello, Edna.

JOEY. Hello.

EDNA. Am I barging in on something?

JOEY. No, not at all, in fact I was just on my way to the library. (*He picks up his briefcase and stands up.*)

EDNA. Oh, it's no good going there. It's closed while they install a new security device. It won't be opened until this evening.

JOEY. Oh. (*He sits down again.* BEN *goes back to his desk.*)

EDNA. Isn't that a comment on our times? Do you know I found a couple of students in the canteen. They actually pretended to have heard from some source or another that there were no tutorials during the first week of the half. What do you think of that?

BEN (*sits at his desk*). *Folie de grandeur*. They must learn to leave such decisions to us.

EDNA. Exactly. I wonder what they'd have to say if we started putting them off for any nonsensical reason that came into our heads.

BEN. Yes, I often wonder that. There's so much about them one never finds out. I mean they come, they go away –

EDNA (*sits opposite* BEN). Do you know anything about my particular black sheep, by the way? His name's Gardner.

BEN. Gardner? Gardner, Gardner.

JOEY. Yes, he comes to the odd lecture, aloof in feathers.

BEN. Feathers?

JOEY. He wears a kind of hat with feathers in it.

EDNA. Yes, that dreadful hat. I wish there was some action we could take about that, too. You don't remember him, Ben?

BEN. I certainly can't place the hat.

JOEY. Isn't Gardner the one you had a conversation with just before the break? In a pub? You mentioned –

BEN. A feathered youth? In a public house? Certainly not.

EDNA. Actually, the reason I asked whether you remember him, Ben, is that you interviewed him for his place here. I've just looked him up in the files. (*She hands* BEN *Gardner's open file.*)

BEN. Possibly. I only remember the ones we manage to reject, like Father O'Couligan.

EDNA. I must say, Ben, his headmaster's report was very unfavourable.

BEN. I'm not surprised. Father O'Couligan was in his forties. The Headmaster must have had him in the sixth form for a couple of decades at least. And frankly five minutes of O'Couligan was as much as I –

EDNA. No, I was talking about Gardner. I simply can't help wondering what made you take him.

BEN. Well Edna, I suppose I must have decided he wasn't fit for anything else.

EDNA. A university isn't a charity, you know.

There is a silence.

BEN. Do you mean for me, Edna? Or for the students?

EDNA. I'm not in the mood to be flippant about the more loutish of our students today. Not with the committee's report on the Senate House fresh in my mind.

BEN. Sorry, what report?

EDNA. It was in *The Times* this morning.

JOEY. I read it. In *The Guardian*. It was very disturbing.

BEN *looks at him.*

EDNA. Disturbing! They completely destroyed the Velium Aristotle. Completely destroyed it. *That* was their way of protesting about South Africa.

JOEY. I thought it was about Rhodesia. The University maintaining relationships –

EDNA. Well, one excuse is as good as another, of course.

BEN. James said it was the Greek Colonels. But perhaps we're underestimating their capacity for direct logical connections. Perhaps they were protesting about the Velium Aristotle.

EDNA. It wouldn't surprise me. I had one or two last term who were mutinous about *The Faery Queen*.

BEN. You mean the Principal? He really should learn discretion.

EDNA (*after a short pause, releases a burst of ghastly laughter*). No Ben you mustn't say things like that. (*Laughs again.*) Besides the Velium Aristotle is no laughing matter. But I intend to nip Gardner in the bud before he gets completely out of hand. I'm not having any bomb-throwing hooligan skipping *my* seminars!

BEN. Any bomb-throwing hooligan has permission to skip mine. (*He gets up and moves towards the door.*)

EDNA (*retrieves* GARDNER's *file from* BEN's *desk*). Well there's no point in my haranguing you. I suppose I'd better take it to James.

BEN. To James?

EDNA. Certainly. Gardner is ripe for a Dean's Report. Oh, I
meant to say, you and Anne must come around soon, if
you could bear an evening in my poky little flat. And Joey, of
course.

BEN. Thanks.

JOEY (*enthusiastically*). I'd love to.

EDNA. How's the baby?

BEN. Oh, very well. As far as one can tell. With babies, I mean.

EDNA. Yes, they are indecipherable, aren't they? How old is he
now?

BEN. He's (*thinks*) six or seven months about.

EDNA. It's wretched of me, but I've forgotten his name. Though I
do remember him as a bonny little thing.

BEN. Miranda.

JOEY. Marina.

BEN. Yes. (*Laughs.*) Marina. He's called Marina.

EDNA. Oh dear, oh Ben, I'm sorry. I always think of babies as
'hims' or 'its'.

BEN. Well, it's probably safer these days. Our ends never know
our beginnings.

EDNA. Any teeth yet?

BEN. Just the – uh – (*Wags his finger around his mouth*) – gums
you know and a few wisdom . . . or whatever they're . . .

EDNA. That sounds most satisfactory. Are you all right for baby-
sitters?

BEN. Baby-sitters. (*Laughs.*) Oh, no problem. Marina's mother is
a marvellous baby-sitter. Anne has simply added a contemporary skill to Goethe's ideal woman. (*After a pause.*) I'm afraid
we are going through what we professionals know as a sticky
patch.

EDNA. Oh dear. Ben, I'm sorry. I don't know what to say. You
must both be desperately unhappy. (*Pause.*) I do hope she's not
in that flat all by herself.

BEN. Oh, we sorted that out. She told me that if I was half a man

I'd leave. But on discovering that *she* was, she left herself. She's
with her mother. Together they make up two pairs. I imagine
Marina is the odd man out.

EDNA. I see. Oh dear. (*Pause.*) It's always so sad for the children.

BEN. Yes, we do suffer the most.

EDNA. Where are *you* now, Joey, are you still in that bedsitter?

JOEY (*little pause*). No. (*Another pause.*) I've moved back in with
Ben again, in point of fact.

EDNA. Oh, so you're both back where you were then.

BEN. Exactly.

EDNA. By the way, did I mention that the little office next to
mine's going begging at last? So if either of you wants a place of
your own . . .

BEN. Thanks, Edna, but we're used to roughing it down here.

EDNA. It's up to you, of course . . . Well I must leave you two to
get on with it. (*She goes to the door.*) If you should clap eyes on
young Gardner, please send him straight up to me on pain of a
Dean's report. (*She goes out.*)

    There is a silence.

BEN. I enjoyed that. It was so graceful. In a little office next door
to Edna. Christ. What does she want him for? (*He returns to his
desk.*) She's got her own coterie – all those boys and girls that
look as if they've got the curse permanently. (*Little pause.*) Her
obsession with Byron is one of the more triste perversions. But
she shouldn't be allowed to practise it with students. She's got
her bloody book for therapy.

JOEY. She's finished her book. That's what she was telling me on
the tube this morning.

BEN. Well done, Edna. I suppose it means another two decades
while she finds a publisher.

JOEY. She's found one.

BEN. She never did understand her role. Which is not to finish an
unpublishable book on Byron. Now the centre cannot hold.
Mere Edna is loosed upon the world. (*Pause. Sits in the arm-*

chair.) Bloody woman! (*Pause.*) Bugger! (*Pause.*) Bugger! The Dean's Report!

JOEY. It *was* Gardner you told me about then? The boy who complained about Edna's seminars in a pub.

BEN. Edna holds her seminars in a pub? I shall have to report this.

JOEY. The one you said was interesting.

BEN. I don't find anything interesting about a student who complains of Edna's seminars. You did it yourself years ago, and you're as dull as they come.

JOEY. Did you encourage him?

BEN. As far as I remember, which is frankly nothing, we had a perfectly respectable conversation about Edna's vagina, its length and width.

JOEY. Oh God!

BEN. You mustn't be jealous, Joseph. The young are entitled to the importunities that you once enjoyed.

JOEY (*gets up and walks towards* BEN). I can't afford to quarrel with Edna. Besides, I've got to like her.

BEN. Because you've got to, doesn't mean I've got to.

JOEY. She thinks of us as allies. If you upset her, she'll blame me too.

BEN. What the Hell are you doing here anyway? You're not lecturing until later. You could have gone straight home and tidied up your room. It's in a disgusting state.

JOEY. The only room in the flat that isn't in a disgusting state is mine.

BEN. Really? Then can you explain why it looks as if a large, dignified and intelligent man has been going to seed in it?

JOEY (*after a pause*). Did you have to use my room?

BEN. Do you think I could put up with the mess everywhere else? You're out most evenings, it's easy for you to keep your room clean. I don't see why you shouldn't learn what it's like to stay at home and fret your way into a drunken coma.

JOEY *after a moment, goes back to his desk and sits down.*

Is *that* your tantrum? How piffling.

JOEY. Look, Ben, I've got this lecture. Can I do some work, please? As I can't go to the library – Please?

BEN (*goes to him*). When will you phone Reg up then?

JOEY. I told you. After lunch.

BEN. Why are you lying about his being out? (*He points* JOEY's *desk lamp directly into his face in interrogation.*)

JOEY. I don't make a habit of lying.

BEN. Which is why you go on being so bad at it.

> There is a shape at the door. BEN *looks towards it, hurries to his feet, as there is a knock. He goes over to the door, opens it a fraction.*

(*Jovially.*) Good morning, good morning, good morning.

STUDENT (*off*). I just wanted to find out about my tutorials.

BEN. Good. Good. Have you got an essay, please!

STUDENT (*off*). Well no, I mean you haven't set one.

BEN. Well do me one for next week, all right?

STUDENT (*off*). Well, what on?

BEN. You must decide for yourself, can't expect spoon feeding. Righto. (*He shuts the door, comes back rubbing his hands.*) I think that's the lot –

> As a shape comes to door, there is a knock. The door opens as BEN *spins around.*

MISS HEASMAN. I found Mrs Grainger, she says she would have come to you on Tuesdays at two if you'd been able to see her.

BEN. So be it. Tuesdays at two with our fingers crossed. (*He crosses them.*)

MISS HEASMAN. Today is Tuesday.

BEN. Ah well, I wouldn't have been able to see her again today, I'm afraid, as she would have needed a week in which to do me an essay.

MISS HEASMAN. Poor Mrs Grainger. But I'm all right as I've

done one. (*She takes one out of her file, and hands it to* BEN, *who takes it reluctantly*.) I haven't put a title on, but I thought 'Hate and Redemption in *A Winter's Tale*'.

BEN. Needs work. (*He hands the essay back*.) That title.

MISS HEASMAN. Don't you want to read it before the tutorial?

BEN. No, you'll have to read it aloud to me. Unless, I tell you what, give it to me now and I'll do my damnedest to get it read before next week.

MISS HEASMAN (*her eyes go to* BEN'*s desk*). No, I'll read it aloud. Two o'clock then. (*She turns and goes out*.)

BEN (*imitates her walk and slams the door*). Bugger! (*He comes back to his desk*.) 'Hate and Redemption' – I told you she was mad. She must be a secret agent, in Edna's employ . . . (*He picks up a handful of essays from the desk then drops them one by one on the floor*.) Hate and Redemption, Pity and Terror, Sin and Salvation. (*Dropping more essays onto the floor*.) Faith and Despair in *Pride and Prejudice*, The Mill on the Floss, Appley and Dappley, Cecily Parsley. (*Liturgically, as he is dropping essays. He looks at his desk*.) Why don't those cleaning women do their job properly? Standards are declining everywhere. Ruskin's char threw Carlyle's history of the French Revolution out with the other rubbish. But then they took a pride in their work in those days. (*He picks up another essay, looks at it, laughs and sits down*.) I should think Reg would enjoy cooking my kidneys. It sounds worse than settling my hash. Anne's mother the mad monk settles the hash of bus-conductors, milkmen, postmen, anyone stupid enough to waste their time insulting her. 'Oh, I settled his hash all right.' She probably got the taste for it after she killed off her husband. I wonder if there was any reference in the coroner's report to the state of his hash. This hash, my life . . . this long disease my . . . (*He begins to read, then lets it slip from his fingers, leans back, picks reflectively at the cotton wool*.) Why the hell did we call her Marina?

I made this, I have forgotten
And remember.

The rigging weak and the canvas rotten

Between one June and another September.

Born in June, May . . . April . . . February . . . November . . .
Conceived in September . . . So sometime in early September
there was what you might call a seminal fuck . . . Where? In
the park once we . . . let me think, beneath the trees.

Beneath the trees there is no ease

For the dull brain, the sharp desires

And the quick eyes of Woolly Bear.

It must be have been our last, we were already fallen into the
sere, the yellow leaf, a flash of thigh in the yellow leaf,

What seas what shores what granite islands towards my
timbers

And woodthrush calling through the fog

My daughter.

JOEY. You do miss her then?

BEN (*goes over to* JOEY). You know, what marks you out as a
repressed as well as a practising pervert is your sentimentality
over children. Marina doesn't need a mother or father, she
needs a pair of hands, to pick her up, change her, put things to
her mouth, put her down again.

JOEY. But later on she might need a father.

BEN. You generally have the taste to let *me* raise the subject of my
ruined marriage.

JOEY. I can't help wondering whether you miss it.

BEN. Only the sex and violence. And these days one can get those
anywhere.

JOEY. So there's absolutely no chance . . .

BEN. Chance of what?

JOEY. Of your marriage reviving. You don't want it to?

BEN. Reviving? It's never died. I consider it inviolate. I'm a one
woman man and I've had mine, thank God.

JOEY. But things can't just go on as they are.

BEN. Can't they. Why not? (*He takes the telephone directory from
his desk and begins to look up a number.*)

JOEY. But supposing she wants to marry again.

BEN. Good God! Who would want to marry *her*?

JOEY. You did.

BEN. That was before she'd been through the mill . . . (*He begins to run his finger down the column.*)

JOEY (*standing up*). Listen Ben, you could be making a mistake about Anne. If you really don't want to lose her –

BEN (*goes to the telephone on* JOEY's *desk*). Your conversation is beginning to sound as if it's been stitched together from song titles of the fifties. (*He begins to sing.*) Making a mistake about Anne – . . . If you really don't want to lose her . . .

JOEY. Look Ben, I'm trying to tell you something.

BEN. Haylife and Forlings . . . (JOEY *looks at* BEN. BEN *sings as he dials.*) Three four eight – owe seven two owe.

JOEY. What are you doing?

BEN (*sits down and speaks into the telephone*). Ah hello – can I speak to Mr Nuttall, Reg Nuttall please.

JOEY (*hurrying over to the telephone*). He's not there.

BEN. Thank you. (*He waits, humming and smiling at* JOEY.)

> JOEY *seizes the telephone, they wrestle over it,* BEN *hangs on to it.*

(*Into the phone, crouched away from* JOEY.) No, I'm waiting for Mr Nuttall please.

JOEY. All right. All right. I'll do it.

> BEN *hands him the receiver.* JOEY *puts the receiver down and holds onto telephone. There is a pause.*

BEN. Well?

JOEY. Do you intend to stay in the room while I find out if he'll have you to dinner?

BEN. Certainly. But *you* needn't stay while I find out. (*He goes to pick up the telephone.*)

JOEY (*shouts*). I said I'd do it!

BEN (*a long pause*). But what *are* you afraid of? He can only say no, in which case I'll only make your life a living hell.

JOEY. Perhaps I'm afraid he'll say yes.

BEN. Well, you do worry for him, don't you, dear?

JOEY. Why do you think it's him I'm worried for?

BEN. Oh, we all know how you worry for yourself. (*He reaches for the telephone.*)

>   JOEY *holds it tight, and looks at* BEN. BEN *laughs and reaches for it.*

JOEY (*runs away with it followed by* BEN). You're a fool, Ben. A bloody fool!

>   BEN *stops.*
>   *The telephone rings.*

BEN (*takes the telephone and puts the base down on his desk.* JOEY *sits down at his desk*). Butley, Nursery. (*Laughs.*) Oh hello James, what? Ah, well I was just pondering those lines –

His rhythm was present in the nursery bedroom,

In the rank ailanthus of the April dooryard –

(*Pause.*) No, no, I'm quite free. (*Little pause. He mouths a curse.*) Gardner? Gardner, Gardner, Gardner. No I don't recall a student called Gardner – What·year is she? Ah! *He!* (*He grimaces at* JOEY. *A shape appears at the door.*) Oh God. Poor Edna.

>   *There is a knock on the door.*

(*He claps his hand over the mouth-piece. To* JOEY.) Block that student! (*Into the receiver.*) He says I *what*? No he must have misunderstood me. I don't recall telling a student . . .

>   JOEY *has gone to the door, opens it, then steps back.*
>   ANNE *comes in.*
>   BEN *sees* ANNE, *gapes at her and turns back to the telephone.*

Look, I appear to have miscalculated, I've got a student after all, speak to you later, eh? 'Bye. (*He hangs up.*)

>   *There is a silence.*

How are you?

ANNE. Thank you. And you?

BEN. Coping with Edna. Do you remember Edna? The one you called a human contraceptive? Do you remember?

ANNE. Actually, I called her a pill.

BEN. Well, I updated you. (*He laughs.*)

Another silence.

ANNE. How are *you*, Joey?

JOEY. Oh. Um, very well thanks. Um, how's Miranda?

ANNE. Marina. She fills her belly and her nappy. She grows the odd tooth. She cries.

BEN. How adult. Except for the odd tooth, one loses that. (*Pause.*) Actually, I've been thinking of finding a new dentist. I know you dote on Tonks, darling, but he's terribly camp. One sits in that chair with one's whole body at his mercy. (*To* JOEY.) Who do you go to?

JOEY. A man in Pimlico.

ANNE. Joey's teeth are always in marvellous condition.

BEN. Are they? Let's see.

JOEY. What?

BEN. Let's see your teeth.

JOEY *grimaces.*

(BEN *goes close, inspects them.*) You're quite right. (*To* ANNE.) They sparkle. Although from time to time I've noticed – (*He hums 'Christ the Lord is risen today.'*)

ANNE (*laughs to* JOEY). One of Ben's marriage jokes. I'm surprised you haven't heard it.

JOEY. Well, I haven't.

ANNE. How flattering for me.

JOEY (*after a pause*). Well, I think it'd be better if I – I'd better get along. (*He picks up his briefcase.*)

BEN. Why?

ANNE. Because he's embarrassed.

BEN. Are you?

JOEY. I've got a lecture.

BEN. He has. On Blake.

ANNE. Ahh. Then he'd better go.

> JOEY *goes out.*

BEN. He's very sensitive. You frighten him.

ANNE. Because he's creepy, and he knows I know it.

BEN. Yes. I've told him. He took it surprisingly badly.

ANNE (*pause*). You've settled down nicely together again, then, have you?

BEN. We have our ups and downs.

ANNE. That's all right then. May I sit? (*She sits on the hard chair in front of* BEN'S *desk.*)

BEN. I went to see you over the weekend, as arranged, but you were out.

ANNE. Yes, I'm sorry.

BEN. Grounds for a scene though, don't you think?

ANNE. Oh, I should wait. (*Little pause.*) I had to see Tom's headmaster about a job.

BEN. And did you get one?

ANNE. Yes.

BEN. Good. (*He stares at her.*) But you look a trifle peaky around the gills – wherever they are. I can never locate them on Joey. Are you all right?

ANNE. I'm fine.

BEN. Good. I saw Marina instead. I expect your mother the mad monk told you.

ANNE. She said it was very quick. Like a visit from the postman.

BEN. I was there for twenty minutes. You'd better check on the postman. Ah! (*He sits at* JOEY'S *desk.*) Well, this is almost as delightful as it's unexpected, to what is it owed?

ANNE. I came to find out whether you wanted us back.

BEN (*after a pause*). Is that an offer?

ANNE. No. It's a question. I'd like the truth please. *Do* you want us back?

BEN. Frequently. (*Little pause.*) But not permanently. Do you want to come back?

ANNE. No.

BEN. We've cleared that up then. I think we're going to get on very well from this time forth, don't you?

ANNE (*pause*). Joey hasn't told you, then?

BEN. Told me what?

ANNE. He's known for weeks. His – what's his name – friend Reg must have told him.

BEN. Reg?

ANNE. Tom told him. At least, he told me he had.

BEN. Tom? Tom and Reg? What on earth have Tom and Reg got to do with us?

ANNE. He's asked me to marry him.

BEN (*after a pause*). Which one? (*Pause.*) You're not. (*Laughs.*) You can't be.

ANNE. Yes I am. Do you mind?

BEN. Yes, yes, I mind very much.

Pause, he pulls himself together.

After all, a man's bound to be judged by his wife's husband. The most boring man in London – you said yourself he was the dullest man you'd ever spent an evening with.

ANNE. That was before I got to know him properly.

BEN. And what do you call him now?

ANNE. The dullest man I've ever spent the night with. But I don't mind. Why should you?

BEN. Because – because I shall miss old Tom, that's why. I'm too old to make mature new friendships with bores, far too impatient. (*He walks round to his own desk.*) They have to grow on you steadily, hours by hours through years on years, until they're actually doing their bit towards holding you together.

Like ivy around crumbling walls. (*Little pause.*) Is that why you want him?

ANNE. Are you going to make difficulties?

BEN. What?

ANNE. About the divorce?

BEN. Divorce?

ANNE. You see, I'm not allowed to marry him until I'm divorced from you. It's the law of the land. Are you going to make difficulties?

BEN. This is humiliating.

ANNE. But deserved. By both of us.

BEN (*laughs*). I'll bloody make difficulties all right. After all, this is liable to be the only phase of our marriage that I shall enjoy. At least since the moment in the registry office when the clerk who handled our contract was under the impression that he was supposed to bind me for a year or two to the mad monk your mother. (*He gets up and faces her across his desk.*) I'll have to have my fun somewhere, won't I? Because after all one moment of pleasure isn't much out of a whole year, is it?

ANNE. It's a moment more than I had.

BEN. And how many moments do you expect from your next?

ANNE. I shan't count them. I'm not in it for fun, you see. I never was. And nor were you.

BEN. Oh. What *was* I in it for?

ANNE. Perhaps you wanted a break.

BEN. Well, I'm certainly getting one, aren't I?

ANNE. Or perhaps you were frightened. But it doesn't matter any more because you're not any more. And I suppose you needn't ever try again, now that you've found out whatever it is you were determined to learn. (*Pause.*) I don't care. Not at all.

BEN. Then you're half-way there. And Tom will certainly teach you to sit still. (*He walks round behind her and comes to face her.*) If you must get married again, surely we can do better for you than that. After six weeks you'll be the two most boring men in London. There are signs already. You're developing a new tone –

a combination of the didactic and the enigmatically stoic – that's more than half-way towards Tom's prose style. By the way, does he know that you greet spring and its signs of life with wheezings and sneezes from your hay-fever? Tom endorses spring. He admires it for its moral exuberance. (*Pause.*) Do you still make little popping sounds when you drink your coffee? No, it's your nose – your nose I've always taken exception to, or is it your mouth? You can't marry Tom.

ANNE. I can.

BEN. All right, you probably can. You can probably do a lot of hideous things. You're tough, versatile and brutal. What I mean is, don't.

ANNE. Why not?

A shape appears at the door.

Well?

A pause.

EDNA (*knocks, steps in*). Can I have a word? (*She is obviously distraught.*)

BEN. By all means. (*He gestures to* ANNE.)

EDNA. Oh, I'm sorry, I didn't realize – I'll look back later, if I may. (*She goes out.*)

ANNE. He's asked me to live with him until we get married. Are you going to make trouble?

BEN. Tell me, when did we last have it off? Was it that time in the park, beneath the trees, or did we have a quick go subsequently, in bed or under the kitchen table, Joey and I were trying to work it out –

ANNE rises.

(*He jumps away, as if expecting a blow, shields his face, then laughs, shakily.*) You're going to live with him *until* you get married, did you say? At least that's a realistic prospectus. (*He calls out, as* ANNE *leaves.*) 'Bye, darling. 'Bye bye, sweet princess, goodbye . . . (*He closes the door behind her and stands pulling at the cotton wool on his chin. He pulls it off.*) Ahh, Butley is himself again. (*Hums 'Christ the Lord', then sings.*)

Christ your breath is bad today

Haa-aa-al-it-osis. Haa-aa-

(*He breaks off, trembling. He sits down at his desk, puts his hand to his face, takes it away, looks at it, touches his chin, inspects his fingers.*) Bloody woman! Bloody woman! (*He feels in his pocket and takes out more cotton wool*).

Curtain

ACT TWO

The office as before. It is shortly after lunch.
When the curtain rises MISS HEASMAN *is sitting on the hard chair*
by BEN's *desk, reading from her essay.* BEN *is apparently asleep in the*
armchair a cigarette in his hand.

MISS HEASMAN (*a pause – she looks at* BEN). 'Hermione's re-
awakening – the statue restored to life after a winter of sixteen
years' duration – is in reality Leontes's re-awakening, spiritually,
and of course the most moving exemplification of both the revitalization theme and thus of forgiveness on the theological as
well as the human level.'

BEN. Level?

MISS HEASMAN. Yes.

BEN. The human *level*?

MISS HEASMAN. Yes. Um, shall I go on?

BEN. Mmm.

MISS HEASMAN. 'The central image is drawn from nature, to
counterpoint the imagery of the first half of the play, with its
stress on sickness and deformity. Paradoxically, *A Winter's Tale*
of a frozen soul –'

BEN. Bit fish-mongery, that.

MISS HEASMAN (*laughs mirthlessly*). '– is therefore thematically
and symbolically about revitalization.'

BEN. Sorry. Re-whatalization?

MISS HEASMAN. Re-*vital*ization.

BEN (*gets up and goes to* MISS HEASMAN). Thematically and symbolically so, eh?

MISS HEASMAN. Yes. (*She looks towards him challengingly.*)
'The central image is drawn from' – no, we've had that – um. 'In
this context –'

BEN. Can you see?

MISS HEASMAN. What?

BEN (*aims his desk light at* MISS HEASMAN's *essay, forgets to turn it on, goes to a hard chair in the corner of the room and sits down out of view.*) There.

    MISS HEASMAN *after a moment, leans over, turns on the light.*

Sorry. No irony intended. (*Pause.*) 'Context.'

MISS HEASMAN. Um, yes. 'In this context it might be said that Leontes represents the affliction that is a universal, and so contingently human evil, and in this sense, the sense of a shared blight . . .'

BEN (*lets out a noise like a laugh, pretends to be coughing*). Sorry. Yes, a shared blight – yes, look, how much longer is it exactly?

    MISS HEASMAN *fumbles through the pages* – BEN *goes over to his desk.*

I'll tell you what, as our time together's drawing to a close, read the last two or three sentences, so we can get the feel of your conclusion.

    MISS HEASMAN *looks pointedly at her watch, riffles through her pages.*
    BEN *picks at the cotton wool on his chin, drums his fingers, checks these movements, smiles attentively when* MISS HEASMAN *looks at him.*

MISS HEASMAN. Ready?

BEN. Please, please.

MISS HEASMAN. 'So just as the seasonal winter was the winter of the soul, so is the seasonal spring the spring of the soul. The imagery changes from disease to floral, the tone from mad bitterness to joyfulness. As we reach the play's climax we feel our own – spiritual – sap rising.'

BEN (*after a long pause*). Sap?

MISS HEASMAN. Sap.

BEN. Sap. Sap. Yes, I think sap's a better word than some others that spring rhymingly to mind. Good. Well, thank you very much. What do you want to do – I mean, after your exams?

(*He sits on the hard chair opposite* MISS HEASMAN.)

MISS HEASMAN. Teach.

BEN. English?

MISS HEASMAN. Yes.

BEN. Well, I suppose that's more radical than being a teacher of exams, for which I think you're already qualified, by the way. I hope you'll take that as a compliment.

MISS HEASMAN. It isn't meant to be one, is it? But whatever you think of my essay, if I don't do well in the exams, I might not be able to be a teacher.

BEN. Teacher of whom?

MISS HEASMAN. Sixth forms, I hope.

BEN. Isn't it more exhilarating to get them earlier? Sixth-form teachers are something like firemen called in to quench flames that are already out. Although you can never tell – recently I've enjoyed reading almost as much as I did when I was twelve. I do hope I didn't slip through their net – it makes one lose confidence. But I'm sure *you'll* be all right. Perhaps books are just my *madeleines*, eh?

> Gravy and potatoes
> In a big brown pot
> Put them in the oven
> And cook them very hot.

MISS HEASMAN. I'm sorry?

BEN. And so am I. I'm not really myself this afternoon, what do you want to do next week?

MISS HEASMAN. We have to cover at least six Shakespeares.

BEN. From what I've heard already, Shakespeare's as good as covered. (*He opens the door.*)

MISS HEASMAN (*holds out her essay*). Could you please write some comments on this?

BEN. It's a good thing to be merciless. (*Taking the essay.*) It comes in useful when dealing with the young.

MISS HEASMAN. Believe it or not, you can be as rude as you like. I don't take it personally.

BEN. That's another good way of taking the fun out of teaching. Good afternoon, Miss Heasman.

MISS HEASMAN. Thank you. (*She goes out.*)

> BEN *stands at the open door, gestures obscenely after her. Then, aware that he is holding her essay, pinches his nostrils, holds the essay at a distance, makes gagging sounds, pantomimes gas-poisoning as he goes back to his desk.*
>
> MISS HEASMAN *has come back to the door, stands watching him.*
>
> BEN *drops the essay onto his desk, stiffens, turns slowly.*
>
> *He and* MISS HEASMAN *stare at each other.*
>
> MISS HEASMAN *turns and goes quickly from the room.*

BEN (*makes as if to hurry after her, stops*). Oh Christ! Bloody girl!

> *He stands for a moment, then takes out an address book, looks up a name, goes over to his desk and dials the number.*

Hello, Kent Vale Comprehensive? Headmaster please. (*Little pause.*) Ben Butley. (*Aside.*) Friend to Education. (*Into the telephone.*) Thank you. (*He puts the telephone on the desk, runs over to a carrier bag, extracts a quarter of Scotch, runs back, clamps it under his chin, unscrews the cap as he talks in a Scottish accent.*) Ahh, hello Headmaster, sorry to trouble you on a trifling matter, but I've been trying to make contact with one of your staff, Tom Weatherley, and it's proving to be a tricky business. (*Pause.*) Ben Butley, Friend to Tom Weatherly, a member of your staff. Do you ken him? (*Little pause.*) Oh, naturally I don't want to disturb him if he's teaching, but I've got a rather delicate message for him, I'd rather entrust it to someone of authority like yourself, if I may? (*Listens.*) Thank you. It's just that could he and I have a little chin-wag – (*Little pause.*) – chin-wag some time about the proceedings – solicitors, alimony, maintenance, custody, visiting rights – always so sad when there are wee bairns to consider – we always say – property, so on, so forth. (*Pause.*) Oh, I'm Tom's fiancée's husband. I've only just heard the news. By the way, H.M., quite a coincidence, my wife that was, Tom's wife to be, Ann Butley that is, might be coming to teach in your school, I believe, do keep an eye out for her, I'd be most obliged. (*He takes the telephone away from his chin feels his chin, makes a face.*) Oh, and there is one other thing, could you tell Tom that he'll have to foot the bill for any ops; this time unless he can get it on the National Health, I've got enough blood on my hands – (*Looks at his fingers.*) – at the moment, and it's all my own, ha ha ha, if you see what I mean. (*Little pause.*) Oh you don't, well never mind, H.M., I don't really think we educationalists should be expected to see anything but the clouds into which we thrust our heads eh?

There is a shape at the door. BEN *looks towards it.*

Love to Tom and Anne when you see them, eh? Goodbye.

He puts down the telephone, stares towards the door, then takes a swig of Scotch, goes to the door, peers through the frosted glass. He drops the Scotch into his pocket and knocks gently against the glass.

Tap tappit, tap tappit, he's heard it before.
But when he peeps out there is nobody there

Opens the door.

But packets and whimsey put down on the stair.
(*He walks over to his desk.*) Or is something frightening him again? Is that why he's peeping through the frosted glass with his whiskers twitching and his paws to his nose, eh?

JOEY *after a pause, enters – goes to his desk, puts down his briefcase and turns on the desk lamp.*

If it's Anne you were hiding from, she's gone. If it's Edna, she
hasn't arrived.

JOEY. I heard voices. I thought perhaps you and Anne were still –

BEN. What? Thrashing it out? Having it off? What would Anne
and I still be doing, together in a small room, after two hours?
She was always succint, even with her knickers down.

JOEY. I saw Edna in the common room. She was just leaving when
I went in.

BEN. And how did she seem? Jovial?

JOEY. No, very upset.

BEN. Ah.

JOEY. Was that Miss Heasman I passed in the corridor?

BEN. How did she look? Jovial?

JOEY. She had her face averted. As if she were in tears.

BEN. Then that was certainly Miss Heasman, yes. Everything
seems to be running smoothly, doesn't it? (*He stares at* JOEY.)
Tell me, what did you make of old Anne turning up in that
enterprising fashion?

JOEY. I don't know.

BEN. You don't?

> JOEY *looks at him.*

She was under the impression that you've known for some time.

JOEY (*a pause*). I did try to warn you.

BEN. Yes and thank you. But tell me, how come that you've
known for some time?

JOEY. Well actually I got it from Reg.

BEN. From Reg? Yes? (*Pause.*) You know I think we're building
up a case here for a conspiracy theory of personal relationships.
Go on.

JOEY (*sits*). Tom's meeting Reg had nothing to do with me. It was
something professional, I don't know what, but they got on
very well and Tom told Reg and Reg told me, and then Tom
phoned Reg and told Reg not to tell me or if he *had* told me to
ask me not to tell you until he or Anne had told you.

BEN. Yes, I recognize Tom's delicate touch there in your sentence structure. It must have been amusing to hear me chatter mindlessly on about my marriage, eh?

JOEY. I tried to warn you.

BEN. But was it amusing? Was it fun? (*Pause.*) Are you going to answer me?

JOEY. Sorry. I took the question to be rhetorical.

BEN (*going over to him*). All right. Let me ask you, then, *why* you promised not to mention to your best friend – is that presuming? – that his wife was being screwed by, while contemplating marriage to, the most boring man in London? Is that question sufficiently unrhetorical?

JOEY. Because I didn't think it was my business.

BEN. Not your business? And how many personalities and dramas over which we've gossiped and whinnied in the past years have been our business? There have been some pretty sticky silences between us recently, and here you were, my dear, in possession of a piece of information that was guaranteed to raise at the very least an amused eye-brow?

JOEY. All right, because I'm a coward, that's why. I'm sorry. (*Pause.*) I *am* sorry, in point of fact.

BEN. Matters of fact and points of fact have been cluttering your syntax since you started going steady with that butcher's boy.

JOEY. I'm sorry because I hoped it wouldn't happen. Now it's a fact and I wish it weren't.

> BEN *laughs, tugs at the cotton wool on his chin and pulls it off. His hand is trembling.*

I'm – I'm sure you could get her back.

BEN. How far back?

JOEY. To live with you. She and Marina.

BEN. That's too far back. Far too far back.

JOEY. Then what will you do?

BEN. Grab my quota of fun, that's all. (*He returns to the telephone.*) I'm working to a very tight schedule. I've given myself a mere

week to get the most boring – and tenacious – man in London
out of his job and home. I'm moving on to his landlady now.

JOEY. Fun?

BEN. Or trouble. I can't remember which I've promised myself.

JOEY. But what's the point of making trouble?

BEN. Fun. (*He dials again.*) Because hounding them from job and
home is no trouble. Local councils, the police, whole govern-
ments do it. Why shouldn't a private citizen be allowed to join
in? (*He waits, then slams down the phone –* JOEY *goes to the door.*)
Where are you going? (*He dials another number.*)

JOEY. The library's open now. I thought I'd go up –

BEN. And hide again? Who from this time?

> JOEY *shrugs.*

From Edna. Yes, it must be Edna.

JOEY. Well, I'm not going to be here when she comes to have it
out with you.

> BEN *laughs.*

I can't help it. *I'm* not going to antagonize her.

BEN. O.K. I'll do it for you. You run along.

> JOEY *looks at him, hesitates, then makes for the door.*

(*Into the telephone.*) Ah, Haylife and Forling, I must say you
do drag out your lunch, some of which, by the way, appears
still to be in your mouth, from the sound of you. (*As* JOEY
hurries to him from the door.) This is Joeseph Keyston, Friend to
Reg Nuttall, if you take my meaning, may I speak to him
please? (*He hands the telephone to* JOEY.)

> JOEY *takes the telephone and puts it down.*
> *There is a pause.*

You see how life repeats itself, with diminishing climaxes.
(*Little pause.*) Well? Is he still out, have you some more
moralizing to do, or are you simply welching on a promise?

JOEY. All right. If you want, I'll cancel Reg. We can go to Bianchi's. Just the two of us.

BEN (*in an American accent*). Cancel Reg? Cancel him? (*Laughs.*) This is a human bean, you're talking about here, kid, not a cheque, or an order of groceries, but a human *bean*! And frankly dear, he's more of an attraction than your shy self, at the moment. All our games together are going a trifle stale, Reg and I may be able to find some new ones.

JOEY. Reg won't be very playful.

BEN. Don't worry. I shall get my fun. Besides, in this bag here, kidneys! Yes, kid, kidneys! (*He waves the carrier bag at* JOEY.)

JOEY (*after a pause*). I'm sorry, Ben. Not tonight.

BEN. Mmm huh. So *you're* not inviting me.

JOEY. I'm not going. We can either eat at the flat or at Bianchi's. It's up to you.

BEN. Well, if you're really not coming then there'll be all the more kidneys for Reginald and myself. What do you think he'll say to that, for an offer?

    A pause.

Don't you care then?

JOEY. No. Not any more.

BEN. You're not breaking off with him, you competitive child you? Is that what you're trying to tell me?

JOEY. No. I'm trying to tell you that it'll be much better if you leave that side of my life alone. (*His voice shaking.*) I can't stop you from phoning him up, you can do it any time, Ben, I'm just advising you, because I don't think you'll get much fun from him, I really don't. I know you've had a bad day already, with Tom and Anne, but you're making it worse.

BEN (*makes as if to dial, hesitates, dials*). You're passing up a chance for a Lawrentian-type wrestle. Can't I interest you?

JOEY. Just remember that I warned you. (*He sits quite still at his desk.*)

BEN. Two warnings in one day.

JOEY *watches tensely.*

Haylife and Forling's? This is Ben Butley, friend to Joeseph Keyston, friend to Reg Nuttall, with whom I'd like to speak, please. (*Little pause.*) Thank you. (*He looks at* JOEY, *grinning, is suddenly stopped by his expression.*) What is it? (*Little pause.*) Joey? (*He starts to put the telephone down, checks himself.*) Hello, is that Reg – (*Little pause.*) Ah, his secretary. (*He hesitates then makes up his mind.*) May I speak to him, please.

Pause, BEN *watches* JOEY, *then offers* JOEY *the telephone. He shakes his head.* BEN *listens again.*

I see. Thank you very much. (*He puts the telephone down, looks at* JOEY.) He's out. (*Smiles.*) Is that a relief?

JOEY. In a sense.

BEN. You'd better tell me about it.

JOEY. What?

BEN. Whatever it is you're warning me about.

JOEY. No. It's nothing.

BEN. Come on, Joey.

JOEY. It doesn't matter. Let it go.

There's a knock on the door. BEN *drops the Scotch bottle. into his pocket.* EDNA *puts her head in.*

EDNA. Are you free now, please? (*She comes in.* BEN *sits down. Very calmly, smiling.*) Now would you kindly tell me what transpired between yourself and this Gardner?

JOEY (*earnestly*). I don't know anything about it, Edna.

EDNA (*still calm*). My teaching, it appears, isn't up to his standard.

BEN. Indeed. Well, I can assure you, Edna, that it's more than up to mine. I know our society has become insolently egalitarian, but I refuse to believe that the gardener's verdict on your teaching will be given too much weight. I didn't know we had a garden – let alone –

EDNA. This is the first time in twenty years teaching that I've been complained about.

JOEY. It's preposterous. You're a very good teacher, Edna.

BEN. All right. Well, let's get this sorted out. To whom did he complain?

EDNA. To James.

BEN. And what did James say?

EDNA. He said you'd promised Gardner he could have tutorials with you. This conversation apparently took place in a pub.

BEN. What? I've had no – well, there was a student, now I come to think of it, but my God I'd completely forgotten – I suppose it might have been Gardner, I scarcely took him in. He wasn't wearing feathers in his cap. (*Little pause.*) Previously you talked of a plumed youth, wasn't it? (*Laughs.*)

EDNA. And you said nothing to him about coming to you for Eliot?

BEN. I have an idea he told me he'd become keen on Eliot. That's all.

EDNA. Keen on Eliot.

BEN. Something of the sort. I suppose I assumed he was after a few tutorials – but really I haven't given him a thought.

EDNA. And did you discuss whether these tutorials are to replace his seminars with me?

BEN. Certainly not.

EDNA. And did you tell him to go to James and explain the circumstances – that he wasn't getting anything out of my seminars.

BEN. Is that what James said?

EDNA. He tried so hard not to tell me what Gardner had said that it was perfectly obvious. He had his diplomatic smile on – the one that makes him look exactly like a rabbit. But I suppose I should be grateful that he didn't encourage that lout to throw my furniture out of the window, or burn my notes. I work very hard for those seminars.

JOEY. We know you do, Edna.

EDNA. I don't expect gratitude, far from it. But I do expect a

minimum of civilized behaviour. And I expect to be backed up
by the Head of the Department and the other members of the
staff when I'm unlucky enough to have a bolshy trouble-maker
in my group.

JOEY. But of course we'll back you up.

EDNA. What happened at the Senate House – it's beginning here.
The Aristotle is just the beginning. (*She sits down, fumbles in her
handbag, closes it.*) But why did they pick on me?

BEN. I don't think anybody would want to pick on you, Edna.

EDNA. Because I'm a woman, that's why. It's always easier to get
at a woman. They think we're more vulnerable. Well, in my
case, they've got another think coming. I haven't finished with
Gardner and like ilk. Not by a long shot. (*Pause.*) How dare he!
How dare he complain!

BEN (*stands up*). Look, perhaps the best thing *is* to let me take him
on.

EDNA. There's not the slightest question of that, Ben. Not the
slightest. He stays in my seminars. That's all there is to it.

BEN. Of course. If that's the way you want it. The only trouble is,
you may not see much of him.

EDNA. In that case, it will be my pleasure to get him suspended.
I've already started a Dean's Report.

BEN. As you wish. It's certainly your privilege. I just don't see
what'll be gained?

EDNA. The satisfaction of causing him trouble.

BEN. Yes, I can see that might be fun.

EDNA. I don't care. (*She opens her handbag, takes out a handker-
chief.*) So you two *are* on his side then? (BEN *looks at* JOEY –
they both go over to her.)

JOEY. Certainly not. I think Edna's got every right –

    BEN *puts his hand on her shoulder.*

EDNA. Leave me alone. (*She pulls her arm away.*)

BEN. Edna. (*Gently.*) I'm sorry, Edna. It's my fault for not taking
young Gardner seriously.

EDNA. Nobody takes anything seriously any more. But Universities were serious once, yes they were. But now they despise them, yes they do, just as they despise me. Just as you two despise me.

JOEY. Despise you!

BEN. I just didn't want you to be hurt – or worry too much.

EDNA. That's precisely what I mean.

The telephone rings.

BEN. Sorry – (*He answers the telephone.*) Butley, English. Oh, um, hello, actually no this isn't too good a time. I'm in the middle of something –

EDNA (*stands up*). If that's James, please tell him that I'm going home. As education has become optional in this College, I've chosen to cancel my classes for the rest of the day. (*She goes out.*)

BEN. Sorry, James. Could we talk later. (*He puts the telephone down, sits on the edge of the desk, has a swig of Scotch, stares at* JOEY.) Bloody woman!

JOEY. So you did agree to take Gardner in, then.

BEN. One of us took the other in, all right. I shall find out later which way around it is.

JOEY. You'll enjoy that, I'm sure.

BEN. I deserve it, after all this.

JOEY. And what about Edna?

BEN. Bloody woman, that's all about Edna. She's lucky to be rid of him. It's not my fault she's too vain to admit it.

JOEY. And all you had to do just now was to keep quiet, and then tell Gardner it couldn't be managed.

BEN. But I *am* managing it.

JOEY. Oh Christ! But what for? What the hell for?

BEN. Perhaps I had a sense of vacancies opening up in my life. I needed to fill them perhaps.

JOEY. Then why don't you do it from your legitimate students, instead of fobbing them off and refusing to teach them.

BEN (*sitting in armchair*). I haven't got any legitimate students.

They're all bastards. Which is my term of endearment for bores. Gardner's interesting. He actually interests me. At least I think he does, I can't remember him clearly and I'll have to see the hat. You interested me once, dear, and look where it's got you. An Assistant Lectureship. Of course I don't know if my interest can carry you through your board –

JOEY. You mean he'll have a relationship with you, don't you? While all poor Edna can offer him is a relationship with Byron, in a properly conducted seminar.

BEN (*hums 'Christ the Lord has risen today'*). Well, Joeseph, what chance your lectureship now? Edna says you despise her. And she's quite right. Toadying is the sincerest form of contempt.

Pause. They stare at each other.

I remember when you stood in this room, darkly dressed to colour up your melancholy, and I had you read a little Eliot to me. Do you remember? (*Little pause.*) Little did we know that a long time away, far into the future, we would be worrying and fretting together about your promotion. Our beginnings never know our ends. They're always so sad, so sad.

JOEY *turns to go.*

Don't flounce, Dappley. It doesn't suit your mousey hind-quarters.

JOEY. It's not my fault you buggered everything up with Anne. You don't have to bugger everything up for me, too.

BEN. No, I don't. I'm doing it as a favour and for fun.

JOEY. I'm sick to death of your fun! (*He goes to the door.*)

BEN. Bum-twitch, bum-twitch, bum-twitch, bum-twitch!

BEN *laughs and* JOEY *slams the door. He runs after him and shouts down the corridor:*

Teacher's pet!

He comes back – has a swig of Scotch, takes the telephone over

to JOEY'*s desk, starts to dial, changes his mind, takes another drink.*
Little pause.

Appley Dappley, little brown mouse
Goes to the cupboard in somebody's house
In somebody's cupboard there's everything nice
Pot, scotch, french letters
For middle-aged mice.

The telephone rings. BEN *answers it.*

Woolly Bear, English. (*Pause.*) What? (*Little pause.*) *Who* would like to see Mr Keyston? (*Little pause.*) Indeed? Yes, yes he's here, just a minute. (*He puts his hand over the receiver, then speaks into it.*) Mr Keyston says kindly send him along to the office. Thank you.

He puts the telephone down, puts the Scotch into a drawer, goes to the desk, sits down, takes out a pen. Feels the cotton wool on his chin. There is a knock. He pores over an essay as there is another knock.

Come.

The door opens.
REG *enters.*

(BEN *goes on working at his essay.*) Minute please. (*Then looks up.*)
REG. Is Joey here?
BEN. Good God, it's Reg, isn't it? Of course it is. (*He gets up, goes over, holds out his hand. As they shake hands.*) I'm terribly sorry, do come in.
REG. Your porter said he was here.
BEN. And so he will be. He just went off to have a brief word with a colleague in distress. How are you?
REG. Very well, thanks. And you?
BEN (*gestures towards his desk*). As you see. (*Laughs.*)

REG. Yes. (*He glances at the desk, appalled.*) Look, you're obviously very busy. If you just tell Joey I'm at the porter's desk –

BEN. Don't be silly. You sit yourself down over there – (*He offers him a chair.*) – and I'll just finish this off, I won't be a minute.

> REG *hesitates, glances at* JOEY's *desk and bookshelves and lights a cigarette.*

(BEN *pretends to go on marking, makes a few exclamations under his breath. Not looking up.*) What brings you down here, anyway?

REG. I just thought I'd look in.

BEN (*writes furiously*). Have to make my script illegible so that they don't find out about my spelling. There. (*He pushes the essay away.*) To check up, eh?

REG. Check up?

BEN. Joey's always saying that if you got your hands on our little room, which is an everywhere, or rather on me, eh? as I'm responsible for the mess we're in – (*Laughs.*) But you should see our flat. Even Joey's room is like a pigsty – naturally, I'm the pig that made it that way. You really must come around and help us out. He says you've done wonders with your little kitchen.

REG. I'm in publishing.

BEN (*puzzled*). Yes?

REG. Not in interior decorating. (*He sits on the hard chair by* JOEY's *desk.*)

BEN. Oh God yes. (*Laughs.*) I'm sorry about that. No, I don't get your job wrong any more. It would be inexcusable. I'm always making Joey tell me about it, in fact.

REG. I know. He's always telling me about having to tell you about it.

BEN. He says you're a marvellous cook.

REG. I'm glad he eats well.

BEN. And keeps his figure, lucky sod. (*Little pause. Gets up and sits on hard chair opposite Reg.*) You know, Reg, I'm very glad to have the chance to speak to you privately – I behaved abomin-

ably the last time we met. I do hope – well, you've forgiven me
for your shoes. I never apologized properly.

REG. It's all right. These things happen.

BEN. But your shoes survived, did they?

REG. They were suede.

BEN. Oh dear. Suede.

Pause.

REG. Look, you must want to get on. I'll go back to the porter –
(*He gets up.*)

BEN. No, you mustn't do that. (*He gets up.*)

REG. I don't mind. In point of fact we were doing a little business
together. He's an Arsenal supporter.

BEN. Good God. Is he really? In point of fact?

There is a pause.

REG. So I can let you get on with –

BEN. Have a drink? (*He goes to his desk, opens the drawer.*)

REG. I don't think I ought to.

BEN (*coming back with the Scotch and two soiled glasses*). You are
lucky. Then you'll really enjoy it. (*He pushes one of the glasses
into* REG's *hand.*)

REG *peers down into the glass, winces at its condition.* BEN
dashes Scotch into it, then into his own.

I understand you've met my friend Tom. Tom Weatherley, by
the way.

REG. I know Tom, yes.

BEN. You know all my domestic news, too, I gather. I only heard
it myself today.

REG. Yes, I heard something about it. I'm sorry.

BEN. Do you detest warm scotch? I don't know how you drink it
in your part of the world?

REG. This is fine.

BEN. Good. Cheers.

REG. Cheers.

BEN. Thanks. (*He drinks.* REG *goes to* JOEY's *bookshelves.*) It's nice
to have some company. These last few hours I've felt quite like
Antony at his close – the air is full of the God's departing
musics. So do forgive any tendency to babble, eh?

REG. No, that's all right. I understand.

BEN. Cheers. (*He sits on the hard chair by his desk.*) Actually what
this whole business has brought home to me is how dependent
I am on my past.

REG (*turning to him*). But it was – excuse me – but it was quite a
short marriage, wasn't it?

BEN. No, I was talking about Joey.

REG. Oh.

BEN. It's as if my marriage were an intermission, if you see. Now
I'm catching up with my past again, which is where I suppose
my future is also.

REG. Really?

BEN. Sorry. I'm being literary. But I always think of *you* as a born
romantic. From Joey's descriptions of *your* past. A touch of the
butterfly, eh?

REG. Really? And what does Joey say to make you think that?

BEN. Oh, I don't know – the way you've pulled up your roots in
the North, what I imagine to be your emotional pattern, your
love of the bizarre.

REG (*pause*). And how does that express itself?

BEN. Joe's always recounting your experiences – for example
with the Gurkhas. You were with them, weren't you?

REG. I was stationed with them, yes. About ten years ago, during
my National Service.

BEN. Exactly. And I scarcely knew what a Gurkha was – I still
tend to think he's something you get with a cocktail.

REG. Do you?

BEN. They must be tough little towsers.

REG. They are. (*He sits at* JOEY's *desk.*) You didn't do your
National Service I take it.

BEN. Oh Christ! Sorry, I mean no.

REG. How come?

BEN. I got took queer.

There is a pause. REG *puts his glass down.*

Oh! You're ready for another one.

REG. No, I – in point of fact, I'd rather not.

BEN. This is an altogether different suburb. (*He refills* REG's *glass.*)

REG. Sorry? What suburb?

BEN. Oh, it's a little joke of Joey's. Almost impossible to explain out of context. (*He pours himself a drink and leans on the front of his desk.*) But how is the world of fiction?

REG. Can't complain.

BEN. Cheers. What have you got coming out at the moment?

REG. At the moment I'm doing two cookery books, an authorita-tive guide to bird watching in Lincolnshire, the only intelligent account of the farce of El Alamein – by an N.C.O. needless to say – and a New Testament Commentary.

BEN. That's your *fiction* list?

REG. No, that's our list for next month.

BEN. No novels at all then?

REG. Well, just one of those historical romances where the hero shoves his sword into assorted villains and his cock into assorted ladies. It won't get the reviews but it'll make us money.

BEN. If he did it the other way around you might get both.

REG (*laughs briefly*). But the point is, you see, by putting that one through we can afford to do something worthwhile later. For instance, I've just made a decision about a novel on National Service life.

BEN. Oh, one of those. I thought that vogue was eight years dead.

REG. No, not one of those. This is something special, in my opinion. Of course it mightn't interest you as you didn't do National Service, but personally I found it moving, witty, gracefully organized – genuinely poetic.

BEN. The National Service? Good God! Those qualities are hard enough to come by in art. It's never occurred to me to look for them in life, especially as run by the armed forces. Cheers.

REG. Nevertheless I expect you *will* be curious in this case. Theoretically I can't tell you our author's name as the board doesn't meet until tomorrow, but if I just mention that he's a comprehensive school teacher – (*He raises his glass slowly.*) Cheers.

BEN (*after a pause*). Well well. (*He sits in the armchair.*) The most boring man in London strikes again.

REG. I'm sorry.

BEN. Why?

REG. It must be painful for you.

BEN. Why?

REG. Because of his relationship with you. It was wrong of me to have mentioned it.

BEN. On the contrary. It was the correct move. Has Joey read it?

REG. Not yet. It was offered to me in strict secrecy – at least until I'd made up my mind. But I can tell him about it now. I think he'll like it.

BEN. That's because you don't know him very well, perhaps. He may be something of a dilletante in personal relationships, but he holds fast to standards on important matters. We once drew up a list of the five most tedious literary subjects in the world. National Service came fifth, just behind the Latin poems of Milton.

REG. Really? And what occupied the other three places?

BEN. The English poems of Milton.

REG. When I was at Hull I chose Milton for my special subject.

BEN. That sounds an excellent arrangement. The thing is to confine him to the North. Down here we can dally with Suckling and Lovelace.

REG. And Beatrix Potter? Joey says you've got great admiration for the middle-class nursery poets.

BEN. With reservations. I find some of the novellae a trifle heavy going. (*A pause.*) I call Joey Appley Dappley, did you know?

REG. Do you?

BEN. And he calls me Old Mr Prickle-pin. After
Old Mr Prickle-pin, with never a coat to
Put his pins in.
Sometimes I call him Diggory Diggory Delvet, when he's bur-
rowing away at his book.

There is a pause.

REG. What did you mean by being took queer?

BEN (*coyly*). Oh, you know, I'm sure. (*Laughing.*) You do look
shocked, Reg.

REG. That's surprising, because I'm not surprised even.

BEN. You don't think there's anything shameful in it, then?

REG. In what?

BEN. Dodging the draft.

REG. There are thousands of blokes from working-class homes who
couldn't. They didn't know the tricks. Besides they'd rather
have done ten years in uniform than get out of it that way.

BEN. Then you think there's something shameful in being taken
queer?

REG. I'm talking about people pretending to be what they're
not.

BEN. Not what?

REG. Not what they are.

BEN. But if people do get taken queer, it's nature we must blame
or their bodies, mustn't we? Medicine's still got a long way to
go, Reg.

REG. Why do you use that word?

BEN. What word?

REG. 'Queer.'

BEN. Does it offend you?

REG. It's beginning to.

BEN. Sorry. It's an old nursery habit. One of our chars used to say
it. Whenever I came down with anything it would be, 'Our
Ben's took queer again, poor little mite.'

There is a silence.

Although I can see it's a trifle inappropriate for a touch of T.B. –
REG. T.B.?
BEN. They found it just in time. At my board medical, in fact.
Why *do* you object to the phrase though?
REG. No, no, it doesn't matter. A misunderstanding. I'm sorry.
BEN. Oh, I *see. Queer!* – of course. Good God, you didn't think
I'd sink quite so low, did you? (*Laughs.*)
REG. I'm sorry.
BEN. It's all right.
        There is a pause.
BEN. Cheers. (*He raises his glass.*)
REG. Cheers.

        Another pause.

BEN. Homosexual.

        Another pause.

REG. What?
BEN. Homosexual. I was just wondering – should one say that
instead of 'queer' – in your sense of the word. Homosexual.
REG. It doesn't really matter at all. I don't really care –
BEN. Do you feel the same about 'fairies' as you do about 'queers'?
REG. Yes, in point of fact. Since you ask.
BEN. Right, I've got that. (*He gets up and moves towards* REG.)
Of course they've almost vanished anyway, the old-style queens
and queers, the poofs, the fairies. The very words seem to
conjure up a magical world of naughty thrills, forbidden fruits –
sorry – you know, I always used to enjoy them enjoying them-
selves. Their varied performances contributed to my life's
varieties. But now the law, in making them safe, has made them
drab. Just like the heterosexual rest of us. Poor sods. (*Little
pause.*) Don't you think?
REG (*stands up and puts his glass on the desk*). Oh, there's enough

affectation and bitchiness in heterosexuals to be getting on with.
(*He glances at his watch.*) Don't you think?

BEN. Oh don't worry. He'll be here in a minute (*Pause.*) How are
things between you two, by the way?

REG. What things?

BEN. No complications?

REG. What kind of complications would there be?

BEN. In that our routine doesn't interfere with your – plural
meaning – routine.

REG. Plural meaning? Meaning what?

BEN. Yours and his. Your routines together.

REG. Ah. Well, it has done, frankly, yes. Now you ask. But I don't
think it will from now on.

BEN (*sits on the hard chair opposite* REG). Then you're beginning to
get the hang of it? Good. Because sometimes I've suspected that
our friendship – going back so far and including so much – so
much of his history and so much of my history which has really
become *our* history – singular meaning this time – must make it
difficult for any new people we pick up on the side.

REG. Like your wife, do you mean?

BEN. Well done. Yes, like poor old Anne. She must have felt her
share amounted to a minor infidelity, really. I speak metaphorically, of course but then I suppose marriage is the best
metaphor for all our intense relationships. Except those we have
with our husbands and wives. (*Laughs.*) Naturally.

REG. So you think of yourself as married to Joey, do you?

BEN. Metaphorically.

A pause the telephone rings. BEN *picks it up.*

Butley, English. Oh, hello James – no, I'm afraid I still can't
talk properly. I'm in the middle of a tutorial. (*He winks at*
REG.) O.K. Yes. Goodbye.

REG. What metaphor would you use when you learned that Joey
was going to move in with someone else? Would that be divorce,
metaphorically?

BEN (*after a long pause*). What?

REG (*laughs*). Sorry. I shouldn't do that. But I was thinking that it must be odd getting news of two divorces in the same day.

BEN (*pause*). Joey hasn't said anything.

REG. No. I'm giving the news. You might say that when he comes to me our Joey will be moving out of figures of speech into matters of fact. Ours will be too much like a marriage to be a metaphor.

BEN (*little pause*). I thought you didn't admit to being – what? different?

REG. There are moments when frankness is necessary. No, our Joey's just been waiting for the right queen, fruit, fairy, poof or homosexual to come along. He's come.

BEN (*after a pause*). Well, isn't he lucky.

REG. Time will tell. I hope so. But I'm tired of waiting to make a proper start with him. I'm tired of waiting for him to tell you. You know our Joey – a bit gutless. No, the truth of the matter is I've been trying to get Joey to bring you around to dinner one evening and tell you straight, so we could get it over with. I knew he'd never find the nerve to do it on his lonesome. But he's kept dodging about, pretending you were busy, one excuse after another. It's worked out quite well though, hasn't it?

The door opens. JOEY *comes in. Sees* REG.

Hello. We've just been sorting things out. Ben and I.

BEN (*to* JOEY). Cheers.

JOEY *stands staring from one to the other.*

BEN. Yes, our Reg has just been giving me the second instalment of the day's news. But then traditionally, because metaphorically, I should be the last to hear.

JOEY (*after a pause*). I wanted to tell you myself.

BEN. Wanted to, did you? And were you looking forward to a subsequent scene?

JOEY. No.

BEN. How unlike each other we are. I would have enjoyed it.

REG (*after a pause*). How did your lecture go?

JOEY. All right.

REG. Grand. Any more teaching today?

JOEY. No.

REG. Come on then. (*He moves over to* JOEY.) Let's go move your things.

JOEY. No, I can't, until later.

REG. Why not?

JOEY. Because there's something I've got to do. (*He glances at* BEN.)

BEN. Oh, don't stay on my account.

JOEY. No. It's something I promised Edna I'd –

REG. Oh. Well, have you got time for a cup of tea?

JOEY. Yes.

> *They move towards the door.*

BEN. Reg.

> REG *turns.*

Are you coming back after tea?

REG (*looks at* JOEY). I don't see any reason too. Why?

BEN. I think you're pretty bloody good Reg. In your way. It's not my way, but it seems to get you what you want.

REG. So far. But thanks.

> BEN *goes across to the carrier bag, scrambles in it, comes back with a package, hands it to* REG.

(REG *takes it.*) What's this? (*Opening the package.*)

BEN. My kidneys. Best English lamb.

REG. You've been done. They're New Zealand, thawed.

BEN. The small, dapper irony is that I've been trying to join you for supper all day – not to say for the last month. May I anyway?

JOEY. Of course.

REG. I'm sorry. We can't.

JOEY. Why not?

REG. Because I've just bought two tickets for the match tonight. From one of your porters. (*To* BEN.) I'm sorry. Perhaps some other time. (*He passes the bag of kidneys to* JOEY *who passes them to* BEN.)

BEN. Thank you. (*He drops the kidneys on his desk.*)

JOEY. Do we have to go to the match?

REG. Yes. It's an important one. (*To* BEN.) But some other time. Now I'd like that tea please.

JOEY *looks at him and leads the way to the door.*

BEN (*watches them*). Reg!

REG *turns.*

I didn't know you supported a London club too, Reg? (*He picks up the whisky bottle.*)

REG. Leeds are away to Arsenal.

BEN. Ah. Well, enjoy it.

REG. Thanks. (*He turns to the door.*)

BEN. Reg!

REG *turns again.*

Will you wear it all then?

REG. Sorry? What? Wear what?

BEN. Your gear and tackle and trim. Have you got it with you?

REG. What? (*Puzzled, he looks at* JOEY.)

BEN. Your scarf and cloth cap and rattle. Your rosettes and hob-nail boots. Isn't that your road, any road, up your road?

REG. I'm parched. Can we compare customs some other time? (*He turns.*)

BEN. Reg! (*As* REG *seems to go on.*) Reg!

REG *steps back in.*

No, it's not customs, Reg, it's you old cheese. Personally I don't

give a fuck that moom and dud live oop Leeds and all, or that
the whole tribe of you go to football matches looking like the
back page of the *Daily Mirror* and bellow 'Ooop ta Rovers' and
'Clobber busturds' or own a butcher's shop with cush on ta side
from parking tickets. (JOEY *laughs* – REG *sees him.*) I really
don't, old cheese. No, what's culturally entertaining is yourself.
I'm talking about your hypocrisy, old darling.

REG. Is that what you're talking about?

BEN (*making a circle round* JOEY'S *desk through the speech*).
Because you're only good at getting what you want because
you're a fraction of a fake, old potato, you really are. You don't
show yourself north except twice a year with your latest boy or
sommat in tow, do you? And I bet you get all your football out of
ta *Guardian* and television except when you flash a couple of
tickets at some soft Southern bugger – do you object to that
word, old fruit? – like me, to show some softer Southern bugger
like him – (*Gestures at* JOEY.) – how tough you are. Did you
cling consciously onto funny vowels, or did you learn them all
afresh? I ask, because you're not Yorkshire, you're not working
class, you're just a lucky parvenu fairy old fig, and to tell you
the truth you make me want to throw up. Pardon, oooop! All
over your characteristically suede shoes.

JOEY (*shuts the door*). Shut up, Ben!

BEN (*walking round* REG). Why, have I upset him? What's the
matter, Reg? I thought you liked plain talk and straightforward
blokes, brass tacks, hard dos and no bloody metaphors. *I* don't
blame you for being ashamed of ta folks, except when you want
to come the simple sod – sorry, homo – sorry, bloke. I'd feel ta
same in thy clogs.

JOEY. Ben!

REG. Anything else?

BEN. Yes, tell me. (*Comes back to confront him.*) Have you had plain
talk and brass tacks about thyself with moom, when she's back
from pasting tickets on cars, lud, eh, or with dud while he's
flogging offal, lud? Thou'd get fair dos all right then, wouldn't

thee? From our dud with his strup? Or would he take thee down to local and introduce thee round to all t'oother cloth caps? 'This is our Reg. He's punsy. Ooop, pardon Reg lud, Omosexual. Noo, coom as right surprise to moother und me, thut it did, moother joost frying oop best tripe and garbuge and me settling down with gnomes to a good read of Mazo de la Roche' (*He laughs in* REG's *face.*)

> *There is a pause. Then* JOEY *makes a spluttering sound, as with laughter.*

REG (*turns, looks at* JOEY). Oh, I see. The information for all this drollery comes from you. Perhaps you'd better sort him out. (*He walks back to the door.*)

BEN. Reg! Coom 'ere lad! You coom and sort me out. Coom on, lud, it's mun's work!

> REG *stops, walks slowly towards* BEN.

Cloomp, cloomp, cloomp, aye, tha's they moother's feet, Reg!

> JOEY *lets out another gasp.*
> *There is a silence,* REG *standing in front of* BEN.

REG. I don't like these games, Joey. You know that.

JOEY (*spluttering*). I'm sorry, I didn't mean . . .

BEN. Going to cook my kidneys after all then?

REG. Is that what you want?

BEN. Ah coom on –

REG. No, I'm not playing with you. So don't say one more word, eh? Not a word. (*He turns to go.*)

BEN (*steels himself*). Ah Reg lud –

> REG *turns around.*

Coom on then.

JOEY. Ben!

BEN. Owd sod, feery, punsy –

REG *hits* BEN *in the stomach, not very hard – he falls to the ground.*

JOEY. Don't!

There is a silence, then a shape at the door.

REG. There. Is that what you wanted?

EDNA *knocks, puts her head in.*

EDNA. Oh sorry.
BEN. Living theatre. Next time around in Polish.
EDNA. Oh. (*To* REG.) I'll come back later. (*She goes out.*)
BEN. For a kick at my balls. Why should she be left out?
REG (*calmly*). But you're pitiful, pitiful. This man you've given me all the talk about. That you made me jealous of. (*He turns, goes to the door.*)
BEN. Still, couldn't take it, could you, butcher's boy!
REG (*to* JOEY). It was silly. You'll have to outgrow that kind of thing Joey.

REG *smiles at* BEN, *and goes out closing the door quietly.*
There is a long moment. Then BEN *goes and leans on the edge of the desk, smiles at* JOEY.

BEN (*touches his chin*). Your bugger's made me bleed again. (*Laughs.*) You're beginning to get little wrinkles around your eyes. Are they laughter wrinkles, or is it age, creeping up you on little crow's feet? (*Pause.*) You'll be one of those with a crepe neck, I'll be one of the fat ones with a purple face, Reg will be . . . (*Pause.*) I was watching you while you were shaving the morning you were going to Leeds. If you'd moved your eyes half an inch you'd have seen me in the mirror. I was standing behind you studying your neck and my jowels.
JOEY. I saw you.
BEN. Ah! Well, what did you think of all that, with our Reg, eh?
JOEY. I thought it was creepy.

BEN. I wonder what your next will be like? Don't be afraid to bring him home, dear, will you? (*Genteel.*) I do worry so.

JOEY. There isn't going to be a next one. At least, not for some time.

BEN. Ho, reely? I think that's a good plan, h'abstinence makes the 'eart grow fonder. (*He sits on desk.*)

JOEY. I'm moving in with Reg.

BEN (*after a pause*). I don't think he'll have you, dear, after your indiscretions and sauciness.

JOEY. Yes he will.

BEN. You'll go running after him, will you? How demeaning!

JOEY. Possibly. But it's better than having him run after me. I've been through that once, I couldn't face it again.

BEN. You love him then, your butcher's boy?

JOEY. Actually, he's not a butcher's boy, in point of fact. (*He picks up his briefcase and returns to his desk. Little pause.*) His father teaches maths at the university. His mother's a social worker. They live in an ugly Edwardian house . . .

BEN (*after a pause, nods*). Of course. Quite nice and creepy. Creepy, creepy, creepy, creepy!

JOEY. I'm sorry.

BEN. Well, thank you anyway for the fiction. (*He sits on hard chair by his desk. There is a pause.*) So you love him then?

JOEY. No. But I've got to get away from you, haven't I?

BEN. Really? Why?

JOEY (*sits at desk*). For one thing, I'd like to get some work done. During your married year I did quite a bit. I'd like to finish it.

BEN. What?

JOEY. My edition of Herrick.

BEN. If the consequence of your sexual appetites is another edition of unwanted verse then you have an academic duty to control yourself. Could I also mention, in a spirit of unbecoming humility, that if I hadn't taken over your studies when you were an averagely dim undergraduate, you'd never have got a

First. Your nature is to settle for decent seconds, indecent seconds, in Reg's case.

JOEY. I know. But those were in the days when you still taught. Now you spread futility, Ben. It creeps in, like your dirty socks do, into my drawers. Or my clean ones, onto your feet. Or your cigarette butts everywhere. Or your stubble and shaving cream into our razor. Or your voice, booming out nursery rhymes into every corner of this department, it seems to me. Or your –

BEN. Shut up! That's rehearsed.

JOEY. Thousands of times.

A long pause – during which BEN *goes to his desk chair and sits – the whisky bottle in his hand.*

I'm sorry it had to be today, what with Anne and Tom. I would have waited . . .

BEN (*in senile professional tones*). Which shows you have no sense of classical form. We're preserving the unities. The use of messengers has been quite skilful. (*Pause.*) All right. All right. It doesn't really matter very much.

JOEY. What will you do?

BEN (*after a pause*). Could you, do you think, staunch the flow of blood? (*He lifts his chin back.*)

JOEY (*comes over reluctantly, takes the piece of cotton wool* BEN *holds out to him*). It's just a bubble. (*He hesitates, then bends forward with the cotton wool.*)

BEN. The trouble with – all these confessions, revelations, clean breaks, and epiphanies, shouldn't we call them these days? – is that – cluttered contact goes on. For instance, we still share this room. (*As* JOEY *steps away.*) You're going to have to live with your past, day after day and as messily as ever. I'll see to that.

EDNA (*knocks, opens the door, smiles*). May I?

BEN. Of course. (*Laughs.*) Of course you may, Edna. It's your turn.

EDNA. Now you'll really be able to spread yourself. It's much more sensible. (*To* JOEY.) I've moved out all my files. What can

I do now? (*A pause –* BEN *sinks into the chair in realization of the news.*)

JOEY. I can manage down here. (*He moves away, goes to the shelves, takes down his books.*)

EDNA. I'm glad I made one of you take advantage.

JOEY *goes out with a load of books.*

I've quietened down, Ben, you'll be glad to hear. But I'd like to say I'm sorry about my – my little outburst just now. I must learn not to be so sensitive. I suspect it's the only way, with this new generation.

BEN. They are rather frightening.

EDNA. Oh, I don't imagine you're frightened of them.

BEN. I haven't enough pride. I shall continue to throw myself on their mercy. (*He goes to* JOEY's *shelves – takes down a pile of books and puts them on the desk.*)

EDNA. They weren't very merciful to Aristotle in the Senate House.

BEN. He had too many advantages. They couldn't be expected to tolerate that.

EDNA (*laughs*). Well . . .

BEN (*watches her*). I haven't congratulated you on your book.

EDNA. Wouldn't it have been awful if someone had got in ahead of me. Twenty years – I'm really rather ashamed.

BEN. Will you go on to someone else now?

EDNA. I don't know. (*She sits on the hard chair by* BEN's *desk.*) You know, last night I played a little game – I closed my eyes and turned over groups of pages at a time – and then I looked at a page. It was in the commentary on a letter from his sad wife. And I remembered immediately when I started working on it. It was in Ursula's cottage in Ockham, Surrey. I was still working on it when the summer term of the following year was over. I finished it during my first week back at Ursula's. I can even remember the weather – how's the book on Eliot, by the way?

BEN. It has a good twenty years to go.

EDNA. I'm sure that's not true. James is always saying that you get through things so quickly. I'm sure you'll be finished with Eliot in no time. Anyway, don't dally with him. Let me be a lesson to you –

BEN (*watching her*). Do you still go to Ursula's cottage?

EDNA. Oh, not in the same way. Ursula got married during chapter Six. (*She laughs and goes to the door, stops.*) Oh hello. No, don't run away. (*She puts her head back in.*) Mr Gardner's here.

BEN. Oh! Right.

EDNA. Will you go in, Mr Gardner. (*She goes out.*)

> GARDNER *comes in. He is wearing a hat with feathers in it, a white Indian shirt, sandals, no socks.*

BEN (*stares blankly ahead, then looks at him*). Well Mr Gardner – you're here for your Eliot.

GARDNER. Yes please.

BEN. Tell me, what *did* I say in the pub?

GARDNER. Well, I told you I couldn't stand Miss Shaft's seminars and you told me I was interesting enough to do Eliot, and that I ought to go and see James. You said he'd pass the buck back to you because whenever he had a problem he converted it straight into a buck and passed it. Actually, you called him Cottontail.

BEN. Did I? (*After a pause, he smiles.*) And here we both wonderfully are.

GARDNER. Yes. (*Smiles.*) Thank God.

BEN. Well let's get going. (*He goes to the shelf, gets a copy of Eliot, brings it back.*) Can you start by reading me a passage, please. Don't worry if you can't understand it yet. (*He hands him the book, open.*) There. Do you mind?

GARDNER. No, I'd like that. (*He sits on the hard chair by* BEN's *desk.*)

JOEY (*comes in*). Oh sorry. (*He goes to his desk and begins to pack the contents of the drawers.*)

BEN. This is Mr Gardner, celebrated so far for his hat. Do you like it?

JOEY. Of its style.

BEN. Once – some years ago – I taught Mr Keyston. During our first tutorial we spent a few minutes discussing his clothes. Then he read me some Eliot. Today I'm actually wearing his socks. Those are the key points in a relationship that now goes mainly back.

JOEY (*opening drawers*). So you see, Mr Gardner, you'd better be careful. If you value your socks.

GARDNER (*looks at his feet : he is not wearing socks*).

> BEN *and* JOEY *look at* GARDNER's *feet, then* JOEY *goes on putting papers into his briefcase.*

BEN. Please begin.

GARDNER (*reads*). 'In that open field
If you do not come too close, if you do not come too close,
On a summer midnight, you can hear the music
Of the weak pipe and the little drum
And see them dancing around the bonfire
The association of man and woman
In daunsinge, signifying matrimonie –
A dignified and commodious sacrament.

> JOEY *finished clearing, looks at* GARDNER.

Two and two, necessarye coniunction,
Holding eche other by the hand or the arm
Whiche betokeneth concorde. Round and round the fire.

> JOEY *looks towards* BEN, *they exchange glances, then* BEN *looks away,* JOEY *goes out, closing the door gently.*

Leaping through the flames, or joined in circles,
Rustically solemn or in rustic laughter

Lifting heavy feet in clumsy shoes,
Earth feet, loam feet, lifted in country mirth
Mirth of those long since – '

BEN. So you're Gardner, are you?

GARDNER (*stops, looks at him in surprise. Smiles*). Yes.

BEN. Ninny Nanny Netticoat,
    In a white petticoat,
    With a red nose, –
    The longer he stands,
    The shorter he grows.

GARDNER. What?

BEN. I'm moving on, Mr Gardner. I'm breaking new ground.

GARDNER. Oh. (*He laughs.*)

BEN. Furthermore, I hate your hat.

GARDNER. I'm sorry.

BEN. Did you wear it when you bombed the Velium Aristotle? And are you going to wear it for your raids on *Dappley* and *Parsley* eh?

GARDNER. What?

BEN. It won't do you any good. Aristotle in his Velium stood alone, vulnerable, unreadable and so unread. But *Dappley* and *Parsley* are scattered in nursery consciousnesses throughout the land. They can still be tongued with fire.

GARDNER. What are you talking about? – I wasn't anywhere near the Senate House when that happened. I don't even know what it was about, properly.

BEN. No, you're a personal relationships type of chappie, I can sense that. Please go away. Go back to Miss Shaft.

GARDNER. What? But I can't – after all that trouble –

BEN. Trouble for you, fun for me. Go away, Gardner, and take your plumage with you, I don't want to start again. It's all been a ghastly mistake. I don't find you interesting, any more. You're not what I mean at all, not what I mean at all. I'm too old to play with the likes of you.

GARDNER *puts the Eliot down, goes out.* BEN *puts the book back, sits at the desk, turns off the desk lamp and tries feebly three times to turn it on again.*

Curtain.

Methuen's Modern Plays

EDITED BY JOHN CULLEN AND GEOFFREY STRACHAN

Max Frisch	*The Fire Raisers*
	Andorra
Jean Giraudoux	*Tiger at the Gates*
Simon Gray	*Spoiled*
	Butley
Peter Handke	*Offending the Audience and Self-Accusation*
	Kaspar
	The Ride Across Lake Constance
Rolf Hochhuth	*The Representative*
Heinar Kipphardt	*In the Matter of J. Robert Oppenheimer*
Arthur Kopit	*Chamber Music and other plays*
	Indians
Jakov Lind	*The Silver Foxes are Dead and other plays*
David Mercer	*On the Eve of Publication*
	After Haggerty
	Flint
	The Bankrupt and other plays
	Duck Song
John Mortimer	*The Judge*
	Five Plays
	Come as You Are
	A Voyage Round my Father
	Collaborators
Joe Orton	*Crimes of Passion*
	Loot
	What the Butler Saw
	Funeral Games and The Good and Faithful Servant
	Entertaining Mr Sloane
Harold Pinter	*The Birthday Party*
	The Room and The Dumb Waiter
	The Caretaker
	A Slight Ache and other plays
	The Collection and The Lover
	The Homecoming
	Tea Party and other plays
	Landscape and Silence
	Old Times
David Selbourne	*The Damned*
Jean-Paul Sartre	*Crime Passionnel*
Wole Soyinka	*Madmen and Specialists*
	The Jero Plays
Boris Vian	*The Empire Builders*
Peter Weiss	*Trotsky in Exile*
Theatre Workshop and Charles Chilton	*Oh What a Lovely War*
Charles Wood	*'H'*
	Veterans
Carl Zuckmayer	*The Captain of Köpenick*